John Pritchard was Bishop of Ox[...]
in 2014. He was formerly Bishop o[...]
Archdeacon of Canterbury. He ha[...] parishes in
Birmingham and Taunton, and was Warden of Cranmer Hall,
Durham. Other books by the author include *The Intercessions
Handbook, Beginning Again, How to Pray, How to Explain Your
Faith, The Life and Work of a Priest, Living Jesus, God Lost and
Found, Living Faithfully* and *Ten*.

SOMETHING MORE

*Encountering the beyond
in the everyday*

John Pritchard

First published in Great Britain in 2016

Society for Promoting Christian Knowledge
36 Causton Street
London SW1P 4ST
www.spck.org.uk

British Library Cataloguing-in-Publication Data
A catalogue record for this book is available from the British Library

ISBN 978–0–281–07352–8
eBook ISBN 978–0–281–07353–5

Typeset by Graphicraft Limited, Hong Kong
First printed in Great Britain by Ashford Colour Press
Subsequently digitally printed in Great Britain

eBook by Graphicraft Limited, Hong Kong

Produced on paper from sustainable forests

Contents

————◆·◆·◆————

Contents

1

'Is there more to life than meets the eye?'

The beyond in the everyday

I was lying in the recovery ward of a London hospital after a small operation. I was under instruction to lie completely flat, and consequently was finding it difficult to speak coherently – even more so than usual. Nevertheless, I found out that one of the nurses looking after me was from Canada and had spent four years wandering the world, including walking the 600 miles of the Camino to Santiago de Compostela in northern Spain. She seemed like a feisty young woman with a spirit of curiosity and courage.

'What do you do?' she asked. Resisting the urge to say 'Suffer,' I managed, 'I teach and write.' Admitting to being a bishop seemed a bit pompous. 'Oh,' she said, 'what are you going to write next?' I explained in my strangled voice that I hoped to write a book about catching glimpses of God in everyday life, starting from the supposition that for most people under 35 in the West, traditional religious language has gone cold. Her ears pricked up and we talked a bit more about the project. Eventually she had to go and look after other people more deserving than me, and I had to recover from being a half-wit in a cream-coloured gown who talked as if he had a dummy in his mouth. As she left she said, 'I'm glad we met. I'll be looking out for that book.'

Well, this is that book. And it does indeed start from the assumption that the language of the Church that sustained and shaped western culture for well over a thousand years has more or less hit the buffers for many of us. Somehow we've poured water on the burning bush and all we're left with are wet ashes. The entire Christian world-view is probably a foreign country to my nurse. Words such as salvation, redemption, atonement, sacrament, etc. are probably not in your everyday dictionary either. We need another language to do justice to whatever it is that we mean when we use the word 'spiritual'.

So I write for those whom one writer calls 'a wider and more miscellaneous [audience] made up of seekers and doubters, opinionated rationalists, religious romantics, disillusioned ex-Church of Englanders, church musicians, thinkers about the universe, and those who dip their toes in and out of the Christian sea'.[1] But I also write for myself (don't writers always do that?). I write for those times when I lose the clarity of revealed faith and need to approach the mysterious jigsaw by a longer, more tentative route. What are the hints and guesses in my own experience that nudge me towards the 'something more' of faith? I think there are probably many faithful churchgoers whose thinking runs along the same lines and who, for preference, would approach the faith rather more speculatively. I hope the book might therefore be useful for home groups as well, and there are group questions at the end. The 'Taking it further' section in each chapter might also be a prompt for discussion.

Francis Spufford, in his lively book *Unapologetic*, describes the situation in Britain in vivid language:

> Most people don't have a God-shaped space in their minds, waiting to be filled, or the New Atheist counterpart, a lack-of-God-shaped space, filled with the swirly, pungent vapours of polemic. Most people's lives provide them with a full range of loves and hates and joys and despairs, and a moral framework by which to understand them, and a place for awe and transcendence, without any need for religion. Believers are the people touting a solution without a problem, and an embarrassing solution too, a really damp-palmed, wide-smiling, can't-dance solution. In an anorak.[2]

But that isn't the whole story, and that's what I want to write about. The situation in Britain is more complex than at first appears. Linda Woodhead has been conducting extensive country-wide research on the state of religion in modern Britain for some time, and she sums it up like this:

> What we are seeing today is an opening up to mystery, magic, and enchantment in the material world and embodied life. Much of my own research has been dedicated to exploring this re-enchantment as it is manifest in the rise of various forms of alternative or 'holistic' spirituality – the extensive world of 'mind, body, spirit' practices ... Examples of enchantment that emerge from the research include the revival of pilgrimage, the re-sacralisation of holy wells, the creation of prayer cairns on mountains, the 'greening' of mainstream religions, the re-working of various forms of religious dress, charms and symbols, and the explosion of spiritual activities focused around bodily healing. We can safely conclude that God never really went away – but he changed a great deal. He now appears with a thousand faces: as personal Creator, impersonal Spirit or Energy, immanent Goddess, and many more. It is not true that religion disappeared in post-war Britain; what happened was that it went underground and incubated new forms.[3]

The politician Enoch Powell had a neat way of putting it some time ago. He said, 'The nation was once not as religious as some like to believe, nor is it now as secular as people like to assume.'[4] The idea that there was once a deeply religious age when everyone filed gladly into church on Sunday morning is more myth than reality. Equally, the idea that none of us tries to make spiritual sense of experiences of depth and grandeur and suffering and being loved is also a myth. It's true that we're tempted to rush past these deep questions and get on with simpler ones, but the mysterious call of the transcendent isn't so easily dismissed.

I used to lament the tendency of many people I met to dismiss religion with the easy distinction that they weren't religious but they were definitely spiritual – anything but admit they associated with something as banal as religion. Gradually, however, I came to see that much of the traditional language of religion had become too tarnished for many people to use, but that the more acceptable word 'spiritual' gave people a toehold in the eternal search for meaning, and I could welcome and enjoy the new vocabulary as an enrichment of our conversation. The words might change but the underlying reality was what mattered. The question is still, 'What's really going on here?'

So 'spirituality' is very much common currency, even though that slippery word frustrates us like a piece of wet soap in a shower. If we were to try and dry it off and use it we might still struggle to define the word, but I warm to the way Rowan Williams puts it in *Silence and Honeycakes*. He writes that spirituality is 'the cultivation of a sensitive and rewarding relationship with eternal truth and love'.[5] My hunch is that this kind of search (treating each word of that definition with care) may be more attractive to many people than one that persists with traditional religious forms and practices that have crumbled away. If you are someone who feels like that, you know there's a depth to life which comes like a gift and is worth exploring. You're drawn to a more generous, less restrictive spirituality that values metaphor and mystery more than proposition and system. You warm to approaches that emphasize the imagination and are lived in relationship and through active participation. You are the new majority.

So I write in the belief that 'God' keeps leaking into our lives but that we have difficulty finding language to describe the experience. I think many of us have intimations of 'something more', something that might even have on it the fingerprints of a divine Source, but how can we admit that or pursue it further? For what it's worth, both popular surveys and academic research suggest that well over half the population have mystical or numinous experiences at some time in their lives, though they're usually very shy about admitting it to friends in the pub. Some of those experiences are edgy, liminal ones, on the boundaries of our normal lives. Others are embedded in the experiences we have every day, but which occasionally resonate with some melody from far away. The question remains what to make of them.

There may be some believers who read this book and get frustrated by what they see as a cautious tiptoeing towards God. Why shilly-shally around when there are clear answers to offer? But what I'm trying to do is to respect the serious-ness of the doubts of my contemporaries, and to respect the genuine difficulties people have with the conventional language of faith. And I want to invite even the believer to accept that, on a dark night with a cold wind from the north, there's an agnostic in all of us. That's the starting point of this book.

Here's a picture. A boy lost his dog in New York City and was later seen walking slowly up and down the streets of his neighbourhood. His friend said it didn't look as if he was really searching for his dog, just wandering up and down aimlessly. The boy answered, 'I'm not looking for him. I'm letting him find *me*. I'm putting down a trail, and sooner or later he'll pick it up and follow it until he comes back to me.'

Is that how God operates? Does God lay down a trail rather than force the issue, out of courtesy and respect for our free-dom? Assuming God does do this, or something a bit like it, I want to examine some of the starting points, the scents, that might be lying around. These are common human experiences that have in them the potential of 'something more'. For example, *the sense of incompleteness*; what's that about? Where might that trail lead? Or the universal experience of harangued teenagers, hard-pressed politicians and the rest of the human race, that *life's a mess* and we don't know how to sort it. Where can we take this mess? What can we do with our wounds? Or the *need for stillness* in a world where 'fast and furious' seems to be the only speed available. Is there a way to slow down, and if there is, could that lead to the peace we desire? These are the kinds of common human experiences you'll see in the list of contents. My hope is that they could be gentle invitations. No pressure. No dogmatism. Just suggestions that there may be 'something more' to discover.

I've set out each chapter like this:

A few typical quotes These are the kind of things you or I might say if we're in the situation the chapter is exploring. They're intended to help 'engage brain' with the experience in question.

Discussion of the main issues This examines the experience itself, wandering around it, looking at it from different angles, wondering what it might mean.

Key question This is a question that's meant to sharpen up the issue and focus it as neatly as possible.

Stories, quotes and things to think about These are different ways of looking at the experience in question, hoping that different triggers will help different people.

Poems Poets often 'tell it slant' and give us an approach that touches other sensors in us.

Taking it further These are practical ways forward if the experience concerned seems worth following up. The attempt is not to be in any way prescriptive, and obviously I realize certain suggestions will seem wildly improbable to some – while, I hope, not to others.

So that's what this book is about. If it doesn't sound as if it will be scratching where you itch, you could stop here, give it to a friend and go out for a drink. But if it sounds interesting, let's get into it.

And to my nurse in the recovery ward – this is for you.

2

'*Is that it?*'

A sense of incompleteness

------◦•◦------

'Is that really all there is?'

'Surely there must be more to life than the gap between paydays?'

'Why am I always looking round the corner for something else?'

* * *

Sometimes in life it seems that two plus two equals three. Life is OK in an OK kind of way but it fails the tests of ecstasy or lament. It rolls on in a safe, middling register, but it feels as if there should be more. A television programme about the great Live Aid concert in 1985, which raised millions of pounds for the Ethiopian famine, showed Bob Geldof's wife leaving Wembley Stadium after the huge event, and she simply asks, 'Is that it?' The question has stuck with me. Is there anything else, something more, or have we done it all, seen it all, understood it all?

For many of us there can be a sense of incompleteness about the life we're leading. The U2 song 'I Still Haven't Found What I'm Looking For' strikes us as spot on. Some will say that that's simply the way it is; we'll always be short-changed in one way or another. Ernest Hemingway went even further, saying: 'Life is just a dirty trick, a short journey from nothingness to nothingness.'[1] Macbeth seemed to agree: life is 'a tale told by an idiot, full of sound and fury, signifying nothing'.[2] Mind you, he'd had a hard day.

For most people, however, it isn't as bad as that. We're merely faced with the 'something else' of existence, that elusive missing factor, the luminous truth flashing like a kingfisher past the edge of our vision. In the meantime we get on with secondary things, with our habits of low hope. The mortgage still has to be paid.

I remember even at college wondering what it was that would hold my life together around some central value and purpose. University usually entails excess, be it time spent in libraries (unlikely), hours on the sports field, or research on the opening hours of local pubs. But I also wanted to know if there was a locking nut that would hold together all the disparate discoveries I was making now I was off the leash and life was full of glorious possibilities. The question felt worthwhile.

We have many survival strategies, of course. If life seems to be passing us by without much progress in the search for this X factor, we can always turn to the golden goblet of consumerism. We can fill our lives with beguiling extras, some of which are simply toys for the playpen, glossy time-fillers. As we establish ourselves in life, with a job and somewhere to sleep, a group of friends and a wallet full of plastic, we might feel more secure in our identity and have at least a passing sense of purpose. But such clothing can be thin and fragile. A few wrong steps, an ill-chosen friend, one or two bad rolls of the dice and we're again wondering what it's all for. The brokenness might be heavily disguised, but the bandages are beginning to come loose and the insistent question remains unanswered: 'Is that it? Or did I miss the moment when the rules were explained?'

So the tug remains. Is there something I've never understood? Is life passing me by without the depth and purpose I feel sure is there somewhere? A friend of mine wrote: 'For many years I thought Hilaire Belloc was spot on when he said, "There's nothing worth the wear of winning but laughter and the love of friends", but even this satisfaction can only go so far, a pointer towards the goal, not the goal itself.' My friend thought himself free of constraints and lived accordingly, but eventually he ran into the sand. 'Fear began to shred what was left of my conscience. I knew I was free but I found this freedom was causing me to walk in circles in an arid land from which there was no escape except inward – and this path led inexorably to a void in the heart. There were no foundations in my life, nothing but shifting sands: a nothing based on nothing. What was I?'³

The story has a happy ending, but at the time it was as if this good man had a great cast of characters in his life but he couldn't discover the plot. He was successful and popular but he didn't know what it was all for. Today's best-selling recipe books for happiness often seem to contain too much 'how to boil an egg' simplicity. It reminds me of Thomas Merton's comment that we can spend our whole life climbing the ladder of success only to find that the ladder has been leaning against the wrong wall. Nor are we helped by the blitzkrieg of secularism which deters us from asking deeper spiritual questions. Don't let's get simple-minded, says conventional wisdom. Don't get caught by the mumbo-jumbo of religious fantasy.

And yet the questions of purpose and meaning are with us all the time. Philosophers, theologians, and artists of all kinds have given their lives to these issues and offered every generation different paths up the starlit mountain. They have disagreed about the route, argued about the equipment, shouted down the mountain from their varied bivouacs, but the one thing they have not given up on is the importance of the quest. In the middle of the night or in the darkness of a personal crisis we are all our own philosopher. I well remember the teenage angst of wondering, when all pretence was stripped away, what actually *was* John Pritchard? I would look at myself from the outside, observe my finitude, and try not to fear my extinction. What was I, and what was I for?

I don't expect most of us to spend much time each day in hand-wringing anxiety about these questions, but that only emphasizes the significance of those moments when we brush against the questions that hang like cobwebs in a dark, half-remembered tunnel: 'Is that it? Or am I made for more than this?'

I love maps. It started with a love affair with the Lake District and the four Ordnance Survey maps which covered that sacred territory. I marked in white ink the routes I had walked and climbed. I loved seeing the spider-like threads criss-crossing the mountains, reminding me of treasured moments and near-death experiences. These were the journeys that had formed me, giving me the stories with which I had bored several girlfriends, casting myself as a Walter Mitty hero bravely striding the peaks. I have maps of almost every new area I've ever visited and I could happily take them to bed and study them with nerd-like devotion.

Now, however, we have GPS. We don't need maps; we just need a device that will reassuringly tell us we're the centre of the universe, and it doesn't matter that we don't know where we are because we have this little helper to direct us along the right path. This reliance on new GPS technology instead of the old technology of map and compass has completely relativized our place in the order of things. We are now the centre of everything, but at the same time we're often lost, and we have to follow the directions given to us by our hand-held tyrant or we might get lost for eternity.

Perhaps we won't know where we are until we take responsibility for our location and make our own decisions. Perhaps we won't know where we are until we look up.

If we 'look up' we might catch sight of a bigger picture in which our life makes sense. Living alone in a friendless universe can leave us feeling disorientated, dissatisfied, incomplete. Acknowledging that incompleteness could be the start of a journey towards a larger world.

Story

A wandering holy man settled down at dusk under a tree, near a big rock, beside a path, at the foot of a mountain. He was going to spend the night there under the stars, with a stone as a pillow. His evening prayers were disturbed by a businessman who came running up to him in a very agitated state. 'It must be you!' he said. 'I had a dream last night telling me to come to a tree, near a big rock, beside a path, at the foot of a mountain. Here a wandering holy man would give me a priceless stone and I'd be rich for ever. I've been searching all day and I'm sure it must be you.'

'Well,' said the holy man, rummaging in his bag, 'perhaps this jewel is the stone from your dream. I saw it on the path the other day. Do take it.' The businessman's mouth dropped open. The diamond was huge! He couldn't believe it. He carried it home, bursting with delight. But the feeling didn't last, and by the end of the day he was deeply troubled. He tossed and turned all night but he couldn't get off to sleep. He wanted to plan a wonderful new future with his amazing wealth, but somehow he couldn't get that wandering holy man out of his mind.

Before dawn he got up and went back to the tree, near the big rock, beside the path, at the foot of the mountain. He broke into the holy man's devotions again and he laid the huge diamond on the ground before him. 'Please,' he said, 'can I have the special gift that enabled you to give away this precious stone?'

Key question

What would be the 'special gift' for us, personally? What do we think we might be missing (if anything)?

To think about

I'm pleased I made it young. I've now got the rest of my life to do what I really want. It would have been terrible to

spend your whole life before you finally make it, just to
find out it's meaningless. We knew it was anyway, but we
had to find out for ourselves.   John Lennon

Is that it?

Philosopher Søren Kierkegaard wrote that ever since human
beings crawled out of the slime they have conducted an
endless experiment to prove that money, sex and power will
bring happiness in their wake. Yet, he said, there hasn't been
a single case in which this experiment is known to have
succeeded. 'In any other scientific field such a failed experiment
would long ago have been abandoned, yet men [and women]
are still ploughing on trying to make this hopeless experiment
work.'[4]

Is that it?

I was talking with a grieving woman about her mother,
whose funeral we were planning. I asked if there was a
story or incident that illustrated or encapsulated what
her mother was like. After a brief pause she replied, 'When
I was a small child I broke a treasured vase, a family
heirloom. Knowing how important it was I screamed as
it crashed to the floor and broke into a hundred pieces.
But when my mother rushed into the room she appeared
relieved, not angry. Gathering me into her arms she said,
"Thank God. I thought you were hurt."' With tears in her
eyes the woman told me, 'That was what my mother was
like. And that was the day I discovered that I was the
family treasure.'   Dave Tomlinson[5]

Is that it?

Aim above morality. Be not simply good; be good *for*
something.   Henry David Thoreau[6]

Is that it?

Taking it further

Here's what you might like to do if you want to think further about all this:

1 Listen to these feelings that there must be 'something more'. Stay with them and don't blank them out. Try to describe to yourself what they feel like – perhaps write them down so that you've captured them accurately and can examine them fully over time.
2 Think of your life in terms of a 24-hour clock. What time of day or night does it feel like for you now? Why is that? How does it feel to be there? What do you want to do with the rest of the day (i.e. your life)?
3 Visit an old place, preferably a quiet one – a cathedral, a local church, some standing stones (Avebury in Wiltshire, Castlerigg in Cumbria). Soak yourself in the place and reflect on your deeper place in the scheme of things. What is most important to you? What would be the 'special gift' that would be preferable to the precious stone of the story above?
4 Read this account of Jesus meeting an enquirer who wanted to know more (John 3.1–8):

> Now there was a Pharisee named Nicodemus, a leader of the Jews. He came to Jesus by night and said to him, 'Rabbi, we know that you are a teacher who has come from God; for no one can do these signs that you do apart from the presence of God.' Jesus answered him, 'Very truly, I tell you, no one can see the kingdom of God without being born from above.' Nicodemus said to him, 'How can anyone be born after having grown old? Can one enter a second time into the mother's womb and be born?' Jesus answered, 'Very truly, I tell you, no one can enter the kingdom of God without being born of water and Spirit. What is born of the flesh is flesh, and what is born of the Spirit is spirit. Do

not be astonished that I said to you, "You must be born from above." The wind blows where it chooses, and you hear the sound of it, but you do not know where it comes from or where it goes. So it is with everyone who is born of the Spirit.'

What does this passage mean to you? Especially, what might it mean to be born of the Spirit?

3

'All you could desire'

What are our longings telling us?

———•◆•———

'I never seem to be satisfied.'

'I never knew I could want anything so much.'

'I don't know what came over me.'

* * *

When I was young our family would occasionally go to the pictures together. It was a rare event and usually magical. The film would be coming to a perfect end, the goodies had won, the hero and heroine had found each other, and I would find myself aching with desire that the world might always be like this, that good would overcome evil, that people would be brave and generous and kind, that everybody would be happy together. I was longing for some kind of perfection, some primeval innocence or wonderful *telos*. I was longing desperately with all my young heart for something beyond, through or on the far side of the imperfect reality I knew waited for me outside the cinema. What was it I was really looking for?

Desire is a universal human experience and sometimes hard to navigate. It may simply be the desire for more money, a better car or a house extension, but the more complex desires are very often relational. It's the desire of one person for another that creates complexity, especially if that other person is unavailable. Such a desire can be all-consuming and even dangerous.

And yet desire can animate our most profound discoveries about the beauty and potential of life. There aren't many people who would exchange the crazy obsession of being in love for the comforts of a night in with *Big Brother* and a cup of cocoa. Tumbling in love with someone is one of the most sublime experiences we ever know and calls out of us some of our highest values and most altruistic actions.

It isn't only erotic and relational desire that can sweep over us. We can be consumed by beauty, overwhelmed by a piece of music, intoxicated by some lines of poetry, transported by the view from a mountain, and each experience can overtake us in the form of longing. We long for something beyond, through, on the far side of, the presenting experience. Evelyn Waugh was on to this when he wrote,

> The books or music in which we thought the beauty was located will betray us if we trust to them [alone]; it was not *in* them, it only came *through* them, and what came through was longing . . . They are not the thing itself; they are only the scent of a flower we have not found, the echo of a tune we have not heard, news from a country we have never visited.[1]

It's this 'far side' of the experience that gives it its particular poignancy and force, a longing that cannot be satisfied but which haunts us with its scorching beauty.

These desires, precisely because they are so overwhelming, can take us by surprise. We have no defences against the inrush of longing and so may find ourselves tossed into temporary chaos. A man once went to a wedding in Canterbury Cathedral and then to the Sunday morning service the next day. He wrote me an email afterwards and in it he said, 'I went out of curiosity, to be in that magnificent building once more. I admit that other than weddings, baptisms and funerals I have not been to church for as long as I can remember. I didn't join my wife in Communion; I wanted to but I didn't understand why; was it just the romance of the occasion? We left the cathedral and I have to admit I just sobbed. There are many reasons [sic] in my life that just came to the surface with a surge. I needed to talk with my wife and, more importantly, express how I truly felt. I don't know whether I've found religion once more; it's too early to say and I'm a cynical devil at the best of times. However, something magical happened to me last weekend.'

Unexpected tears are one of the ways we respond physically to a flood of emotion and desire. But what's going on? What was this good man on the edge of? What was he searching for?

I've been writing of 'high-octane' desires, but most of us, of course, experience many everyday longings. A young person might long to get into a school team or a particular university. An ambitious employee might long for promotion or recognition. A weary senior executive might long for retirement and an end to the relentless pressure. Most of us desire better lives, defining 'better' in hundreds of ways, but seeing it as a distant objective that basks in sunshine on a hilltop far away. We long for better relationships, more success in pet projects, more hope on Monday mornings. Desire is an essential element of our humanness; it keeps us focused, directed and motivated. But even these more tangible longings may point to a more all-encompassing goal, one that lies beyond the here and now. What are we really longing for?

This longing for 'something beyond' can even accost those with firmly rational interpretations of reality. Atheist philosopher A. C. Grayling has spoken of 'the lingering splinter in the mind . . . a sense of yearning for the absolute'.[2] And these words were found on the desk of his illustrious predecessor Bertrand Russell after his death: 'The centre of me is always and eternally a terrible pain – a curious, wild pain – a searching for something transfigured and infinite. The beatific vision – God. I do not find it. I do not think it is to be found – but the love of it is my life.'[3] This love of an elusive Ultimate is a common human theme, but its universality doesn't make it any easier to capture.

There are times when we feel ourselves to be on the brink of immensity but with no way of taking hold of it, and no way of expressing it adequately either. The usual word for the experience is transcendence. Grayling and Russell can hardly have been clearer in their atheism, but, as honest thinkers, neither can they deny the powerful attraction of the absolute as the end of their exploring. So it is for many of us. It's as if there's a powerful magnet operating somewhere and every so often we get caught in its powerful attraction, but we're not sure whether to resist or submit. St Augustine understood this experience, and he had an explanation for it as well. He famously addressed God, 'You have made us for yourself, O Lord, and our heart is restless until it finds its rest in you.'[4] According to Augustine our restless longings have an ultimate goal and destination. My longing for another person is part of my greater longing for union with the divine source of life. My emotional response to holding the miracle of a just-born child is a pointer to the marvel of the Creator. My search for a home for my deepest desires is an echo of the soul's desire for God.

Perhaps this is humanity's true destiny, and just occasionally we get a shock as we touch the electric fence. Trying to describe an adventurous new production, theatre designer Thierry Mugler said, 'Humanity is diverse. Yet despite that diversity everyone is searching, searching for love, searching for the sublime, trying to praise the cosmos.'[5]

Is everyone searching? It's an open question. But many are, and are not sure where to look in a culture starved of the spiritual, or at least starved of encouragement to look in that direction. So people are left to fend for themselves, to knock up a meal from whatever they can find in the fridge. Our culture doesn't really want to give house-room to such fanciful ideas as our hearts being restless until they find their rest in God. Nor does it want to encourage too much emotion when transcendence turns up uninvited. These overwhelming experiences of longing that reduce us to jelly are often greeted with the put-down 'you're just being emotional'. Now, I'm someone who has to admit to experiencing blurred vision when watching the TV advert for John Lewis at Christmas, so I'm not exactly a rational witness here. But it seems to me there are deeper issues involved in these powerful emotional responses. Emotion is usually a reliable indicator that something significant is going on.

The best response to these deep desires is perhaps not to ask for less intensity but for more, to deepen those desires until nothing but the divine can satisfy them. It's not the desire that's the problem; it's only disordered desire that needs sorting. Speaking of the problem of lust, for example, Kingsley Amis said that he felt as if he had spent most of his adult life chained to a lunatic. So we have to re-order and re-direct those desires back to their proper course, to channel them into paths of creativity and mutual benefit where love is rich but not dangerous. And perhaps, as well, to recognize that there may be an eternal destination for these deep desires of the heart. Desire may be giving us a glimpse of a world crackling with energy where the dots are truly joined up and everything is connected. That world just might have the scent of eternity.

Key question

What are our longings? What are we reaching out for? Are we looking for something, or is something looking for us?

To think about

As I stood beside a flowering currant bush on a summer day there suddenly arose in me without warning, and as if from a depth not of years but of centuries, the memory of that earlier morning at the Old House when my brother had brought his toy garden into the nursery. It is difficult to find words strong enough for the sensation which came over me; Milton's 'enormous bliss' of Eden comes somewhere near it. It was a sensation, of course, of desire; but desire for what? Not, certainly, for a biscuit-tin filled with moss, nor even for my own past. 'Oh, I desire too much' [in Greek] – and before I knew what I desired, the desire itself was gone, the whole glimpse withdrawn, the world turned commonplace again, or only stirred by a longing for the longing that had just ceased. It had taken only a moment of time; and in a certain sense everything else that had ever happened to me was insignificant by comparison.   C. S. Lewis, *Surprised by Joy*[6]

Late have I loved you, O Beauty ever ancient, ever new, late have I loved you! You were within me, but I was outside, and it was there that I searched for you. In my unloveliness I plunged into the lovely things which you created. You were with me, but I was not with you. Created things kept me from you; yet if they had not been in you they would have not been at all. You called, you shouted, and you broke through my deafness. You flashed, you shone, and you dispelled my blindness. You breathed your fragrance on me; I drew in breath and now I pant for you. I have tasted you, now I hunger and thirst for more. You touched me, and I burned for your peace.

St Augustine, *Confessions*[7]

Taking it further

If you'd like to think further about these longings and how they fit in, here are some things you might like to do:

1 Just brooding inside ourselves goes nowhere; you might try taking your experiences into a larger place to gain some perspective. Go for a long walk, perhaps to the coast or a hill

or mountain. Or if it's not possible to go out, watch a spectacular nature programme on television. Let the longing find its rightful place in the vast scale of nature's beauty. Then see what happens to those longings, and what decisions you make about them.

2 Start a journal to record some of your deepest thoughts and feelings. A journal is somewhere you can be as honest as your defences allow, and which no one else is allowed to see unless you want them to.

3 Read Psalm 139, which reveals a God who knows us through and through and from whom there's no need to hide anything. Here are the first few verses:

> O LORD, you have searched me and known me.
> You know when I sit down and when I rise up;
> You discern my thoughts from far away.
> You search out my path and my lying down,
> and are acquainted with all my ways.
> Even before a word is on my tongue,
> O LORD, you know it completely.
> You hem me in, behind and before,
> and lay your hand upon me.
> Such knowledge is too wonderful for me;
> it is so high that I cannot attain it.
> Where can I go from your spirit?
> Or where can I flee from your presence?
> If I ascend to heaven, you are there;
> If I make my bed in Sheol, you are there.
> If I take the wings of the morning
> and settle at the farthest limits of the sea,
> even there your hand shall lead me,
> and your right hand shall hold me fast.

4

'Life couldn't hold any more'
Being fully alive

———•◆•———

'I've never felt more alive in my life.'

'I felt I could do anything.'

'How can I follow that!'

* * *

There must have been times when your life, like mine, has felt full to bursting. When you felt so overwhelmingly complete you either wanted to dance and sing (which in my case would have been highly embarrassing) or were reduced to silent amazement. When each of our grandchildren has been born I've felt such an extraordinary depth of love, and such an instinct to protect at all costs, that I've been knocked sideways. Here was a beautiful new person, one who had never existed before, presented to the world. I would have given my life to keep that child safe.

I once went trekking in the Annapurna range in the Himalayas. I had hit staid midlife and thought the opportunity had gone, but when I stood at dawn in the Annapurna Sanctuary, surrounded by ten magnificent, silent peaks of around 7,000 metres, I felt as if life couldn't hold anything more. The scale and majesty of those mountains was breathtaking and filled my soul. It was the same when I managed the Three Peaks Challenge – the highest mountains in England, Scotland and Wales – in 48 hours. (You're supposed to do it in 24 hours but I was over 50 – cut me some slack!) The feeling of satisfaction, of totality, as we stood on the top of Snowdon at 7 a.m. and phoned our partners, was both bizarre ('Everyone sleep well?') and wonderful.

These are ultimate moments. Standing in silent, snowy woods on a winter's day. Holding a much-loved partner in the dark. Watching the sun retreat over the horizon after a magical day on the coastal path. These are the kind of memories that call down the stars.

These shining moments remind us that the world is a place as rich and exciting as anything we could have dreamed of, and that we should raise our sights beyond a secure pension and wanting to be a world authority on paper clips. They're utterly remote from the humdrum times when life seems to be experienced in 26 shades of vanilla. The other end of the spectrum is a dull, clunky old reality in which home life is monotonous, the daily grind is soulless, and evening television has the intellectual reach of a crisp packet. We know, somewhere inside, that this is not what we were made for.

The beauty of life is that sometimes we just get connected. Everything lines up and the electricity flows. Roger Bannister, the first athlete to run a four-minute mile, wrote in the preface to his autobiography:

> I remember vividly a moment as a child when I stood barefoot on firm dry sand by the sea. The air had a special quality. The sound of breakers on the shore shut out all others. I looked up at the clouds, like great white-sailed galleons, chasing proudly inland. I looked down at the regular ripples on the sand and could not absorb so much beauty. I was taken aback – each of the myriad particles of sand was perfect in its way. I looked more closely, hoping perhaps that my eyes might detect some flaw. But for once there was nothing to detract from this feeling of closeness to nature. In this supreme moment I leapt in sheer joy and started to run. I was startled and frightened by the tremendous excitement that so few steps could create. I glanced around

uneasily to see if anyone was watching. A few more steps –
self-consciously now and firmly gripping the original
excitement. I was running now, and a fresh rhythm entered
my body. I was no longer conscious of my movement. I
discovered a new unity with nature. I had found a new
source of power – a source I never dreamt existed.[1]

That experience of being completely aligned with nature/your
best self/God is a thrilling moment that comes to us as a gift
and to which we can only surrender in silent gratitude.

Or not so silent. I had a friend at college who would occasionally come out with an extraordinary cry of joy, rather like
an old-fashioned kettle blowing its top. He simply couldn't
contain himself any longer; life was just too good. Come to
think of it, 'blowing its top' was just what was happening – my
friend was boiling over with life. The writer Emile Zola said,
'If you ask me what I came into this life to do, I will tell you;
I came to live out loud.'[2]

This fullness of life is often experienced as an overwhelming
sense of connection. Instead of seeing life from inside our
own bubble we become aware of the web of humanity all
around us. Instead of feeling fragmented and on our own we
feel marvellously stitched into the fabric of creation, at one
with everything around us.

Thomas Merton, the Trappist monk whose incisive writing
from his hermitage in Kentucky has inspired millions of hungry
seekers, was in a local town one day to see about some printing
for the monastery when he was overcome with a sense of connection to everything around him. He wrote:

In Louisville at the corner of Fourth and Walnut, in the
centre of the shopping district, I was suddenly overwhelmed
with the realization that I loved all those people, that they
were mine and I theirs, that we could not be alien to one
another even though we were total strangers. It was like
waking from a dream of separateness, of spurious self-

isolation in a special world, the world of renunciation and supposed holiness.[3]

This is important. We are not made for separate, autonomous living. We are made to connect, to share, participate, engage, love. We're told that a child brought up in total isolation becomes feral. Thomas Merton caught a glimpse of a more profound reality when he saw through the diaphanous curtain of normality. He glimpsed the reality that always exists but is little inhabited – that we are all connected and can't flourish without each other. Underneath the world's oceans all land masses are connected in a continuous landscape under the sea. So are we all, but only rarely do we catch a vision of that unity; we prefer to divide, fight, assert differences, create boundaries. And so destroy ourselves.

Another piece of learning from Merton's experience is that we don't need to be in exceptional places (Annapurna, the Three Peaks, a coastal path) to know this contentment of 'life-full-ness'. The ordinary can be transfigured: 'the corner of Fourth and Walnut'. This is good news because there is, by definition, much more ordinary stuff in life than extraordinary, and it's good to know that we can experience delight on many very ordinary occasions and not just when we've cashed in a pension and gone off on a midlife gap year.

In his remarkable book *The Solace of Fierce Landscapes*, Belden Lane describes a meeting with the lama of a monastery high on the Tibetan plateau. The lama was asked if he was happy there, where he'd lived for years in seclusion. 'Now old and crippled, he would never again be able to cross the high passes to the outside world. With eyes flung to the sky the lama answered, "Of course I'm happy here! It's wonderful! *Especially when I have no choice*."' There's the hinge of the paradox. Can I learn to say the same, here in the caughtness and constrictions of where I am? Seeing this job as able to occasion the holy? Wishing for nothing else. 'Especially when I have no choice.'[4]

The well-worn paths where we have little choice can still be full of joy, the well-used containers may still be full of liquid gold. It's partly a question of how we engage with the everyday and humdrum parts, i.e. the majority, of our lives. There is depth in ordinary things, but only if we notice. If we listen when we wake, both the city and the countryside hum with life in very different but unmistakable ways. When we meet the shop assistant, our work colleague or our neighbour down the road we're meeting a human narrative of joys and disappointments, sun and sadness – the whole rich mix. When we're answering personal emails we're actually addressing someone with a need, however prosaic, or they wouldn't be emailing us. When we watch the news we're exposed to the wrath and wrong of a world out of kilter with itself but beautiful and miraculous nevertheless. It all depends on how we look and what we see. And that feels more like a decision than anything else. If we are able to see our life as deep in detail and colour then so it is; if we trundle through the day resenting its dull predictability, then so it will be.

But there is another, darker experience that has to be recorded in this category of 'Life couldn't hold any more', and that's one that is indistinguishable from terror. A fuller account is described below in the section 'To think about', but Barbara Ehrenreich, a political activist who had long been 'out' as an atheist, writes in her book *Living with a Wild God* about a seminal experience as a 17-year-old which she had been reprocessing for years as an adult, and which she describes as an epiphany 'that seemed to be best understood as an explosion, a calamitous natural process like an earthquake or storm, leaving behind it what is known in science fiction as a "rent in the fabric of time". Something was broken.' She would have used the word 'ecstasy', but only if that included some resemblance to an outbreak of violence. This, and other experiences, led her, eventually, to conclude that the purpose of our minds is 'to condense all the chaos and mystery of the world into a palpable Other or Others, not necessarily because we love it, and certainly not out of any intention to "worship" it. But ultimately because we have no choice in the matter. I have the impression that it may be seeking us out.'[5]

Here was an epiphany that had burst through the normal categories of experience and in some way 'claimed' the writer. This is one of the defining characteristics of these moments; we don't seek them out in order to tick another box in our bucket list, they take hold of us and shake us awake with their depth and power.

The question behind all these transcendent moments, both glorious and terrifying, must surely be about their source. As with all the experiences in this book, that question doesn't *have* to be asked – it's not an exam – and many people will simply delight in those experiences, re-tell them, and feed on them for many years. But for some of us the question is bound to emerge shyly from round the corner: 'What's the origin of such an overwhelming experience, the source of such energy, the under-lying meaning of such a transfiguration? How does it acquire such power? What or who is behind it?'

I was leading a retreat by the Sea of Galilee and had taken a communion service in the most glorious location, with the lake as the backdrop and a sense of Presence that was tangible. Afterwards one of the participants said to me, 'If the entire cost of this retreat had just been for that one service, it would have been worth it.' It was clearly one of those peak experiences, and it made the sacramental connection to the divine Source of all ultimate gifts. It joined everything up: it completed the circuit. A glimpse of transcendence.

Key question

How could we tap into that 'life-full-ness' in a deeper, more consistent way?

Poem: Miracles

Why, who makes much of a miracle!
As to me I know nothing else but miracles
Whether I walk the streets of Manhattan
Or dart my sight over the roofs of houses toward the sky,
Or wade with naked feet along the beach just in the edge of the
water,
Or stand under trees in the woods,
Or talk by day with anyone I love, or sleep in the bed at night with
anyone I love
Or sit at table at dinner with the rest,
Or look at strangers opposite me riding in the car,
Or watch honey bees busy round the hive of a summer forenoon,
Or animals feeding in the fields,
Or birds, or the wonderfulness of insects in the air,
Or the wonderfulness of the sundown, or of stars shining so quiet
and so bright,
Or the exquisite delicate thin curve of the new moon in spring;
These with the rest, one and all, are to me miracles
The while referring, yet each distinct and in its place.
To me every hour of the light and dark is a miracle,
Every cubic inch of space is a miracle
Every square yard of the surface of the earth is spread with the
same,
Every foot of the interior swarms with the same.
To me the sun is a continual miracle,
The fishes that swim – the rocks – the motion of the waves – the
ships with men in them,
What stranger miracles are there?   Walt Whitman[6]

To think about

In the next few minutes, on that empty street, I found
whatever I had been looking for. Here we leave the

jurisdiction of language, where nothing is left but the vague gurgles of surrender expressed in such words as 'ineffable' and 'transcendent'. For most of the intervening years my general thought has been: if there are no words for it, then don't say anything about it . . . But there is one image, handed down over the centuries, that seems to apply, and that is the image of fire, as in the 'burning bush'. At some point in my pre-dawn walk the world flamed into life. How else to describe it? There were no visions, no prophetic voices or visits by totemic animals, just this blazing everywhere. Something poured into me, and I poured out into it. This was not the passive beatific merger with 'the all' as promised by the eastern mystics. It was a furious encounter with a living substance that was coming at me through all things at once, and one reason for the terrible wordlessness of the experience is that you cannot observe fire really closely without becoming part of it . . . I stopped at some point in front of a secondhand store, transfixed by the blinding glow of the most mundane objects, teacups and toasters. I could not contain it, this onrush. Nothing could contain it. Everywhere, 'inside' and out, the only condition was overflow . . . I knew that the heavens had opened and poured into me, and I into them, but there was no way to describe it, even to myself. As for telling anyone else, what would I have said? That I had been savaged by a flock of invisible angels – lifted up in a glorious flutter of iridescent feathers, then mauled, emptied of all intent and purpose, and pretty much left for dead?

Barbara Ehrenreich, *Living with a Wild God*[7]

Taking it further

If you'd like to think further about these experiences, here are some things you might like to do:

1 Keep enjoying whatever it is that makes you feel fully alive. Enter it, relish it, share it.
2 Try giving thanks, to whatever or whoever you might believe in, for whatever it is that gives you life.
3 Think about these quotes:

> It has long been my conviction that God is not hugely concerned as to whether we are religious or not. What matters to God, and matters supremely, is whether we are alive or not. If your religion brings you more fully to life, God will be in it; but if your religion inhibits your capacity for life or makes you run away from it, you may be sure God is against it, just as Jesus was.
>
> John V. Taylor[8]

I came that they may have life, and have it abundantly.

Jesus, John 10.10

5

'Earth's crammed with heaven'

The meanings of wonder

———— ▪•◆•▪ ————

'It blew me away. I was speechless.'

'It was so beautiful I was in tears.'

'I just looked and looked.'

* * *

This chapter and the last overlap in many ways. However, the previous chapter focused on the disorienting nature of an overwhelming experience of 'life-full-ness', whereas this one is concerned with the somewhat more controllable encounters we have with wonder. We're more acquainted with wonder than with those rare moments of completeness and connection. We may be speechless for a while, but our minds can usually process the experience.

For many of us, it's some spine-tingling exposure to the rich excesses of the natural world that does it. I stand baffled by beauty on a vast Normandy beach, with the sand stretching to the sea stretching to the sky stretching to eternity. I lie at night in my sleeping bag in the Sinai desert, gazing up at the staggering immensity of the ink-dark sky, watching a shooting star bid farewell to the universe. I look in vain for the Himalayan peak, only to find, with a gasp, that it's so far above the hovering clouds that I hadn't noticed it. I peer into the recesses of a flower-head (having no idea what flower it is until my wife tells me) and gaze on layer after layer of detailed beauty that defies imagination; why does nature bother? (Sara Maitland says that any God who consents to the number of different forms of insect life that we have on this tiny planet clearly prefers variety to smooth administration.)

According to the Jewish Talmud every blade of grass has its own angel bending over it, whispering 'grow, grow'. And grow it does, with the exhilaration of the cosmos pulsing through it. Rather more prosaically, but with total accuracy, I once enjoyed a Gateshead resident note approvingly that 'a single blade of grass can bugger up six inches of concrete'. We can be stopped in our tracks by both the detail of nature and its grand design.

Design? Why so? William Blake observed that 'The tree which moves some to tears of joy is, in the eyes of others, only a green thing which stands in the way.'[1] It's perfectly possible simply to wonder at the profligate beauty of nature without invoking God. Richard Dawkins and other materialists delight in the loveliness of the natural world simply on its own terms. They have no desire 'to call the green leaf grey'[2] but nor do they want to attribute to it any other than scientific explanations.

And yet it has been the consistent witness of history that men and women have turned in two directions when encountering the fullness of nature's palette. One direction has been to the poetic imagination, where words can overflow the boundaries of everyday speech and forge new associations, enabling us to express our amazement at what lies before us. Think of Wordsworth watching his ten thousand daffodils 'tossing their heads in sprightly dance'.[3] Or e.e. cummings writing of the world being 'mud-luscious' and 'puddle-wonderful'.[4] Could you ever come up with a more delicious description?

The other direction in which men and women have looked to do justice to the amazing things before them is to a Creator. The writer A. S. Byatt has a character in *The Biographer's Tale* who says, 'I was, so to speak, metaphysically baffled by the sea orchid and the eyes in butterfly's wings ... I understood the argument that a resemblance could be perfected over millennia by a flower or the scales on a wing by natural selection – but

I couldn't really believe it. It still had a quality of designed poetry that left me baffled.'[5] This character expresses the struggle we have to give a fully adequate account of wonder. We may, and should, accept all that biological and botanical sciences can tell us about the evolution of butterfly and plant life, but there's still a nagging 'remainder' if we are to do full justice to the encounter we have with the beauty before us. So much still seems like 'designed poetry'.

This is where poets can come to the rescue again, because some of them wonderfully combine their art with their theology. Gerard Manley Hopkins, for example: 'All things therefore are charged with love, are charged with God, and if we know how to touch them, give off sparks and take fire, yield drops and flow, ring and tell of him.'[6] His 'Pied Beauty', at the end of this chapter, is another example. Novelists too may make the connection. Alice Walker in *The Color Purple* has her feisty character Shug Avery say, 'I think it pisses God off if you walk by the color purple in a field somewhere and don't notice it.'[7] Literature and theology often feed off each other when trying to handle beauty.

Of course nature tells a million stories and many of them are brutal. She is unkind to the weak, outrageously wasteful, and unforgiving to those who stand in her way. It's not all wonderful. Perhaps it's not entirely heretical for the believer to say that this world is a kind of 'first sketch' of the new creation that will finally be revealed. It has perfections because it's 'made' by God, but it has imperfections because it isn't God.

It also needs to be said that I have here only associated wonder with observable things in nature, and there are a million other amazements in this world that take our breath away. Take the miracle (why not use the word?) of DNA. Each cell of your body and mine contains a total of two metres of DNA. Those molecules of DNA are very tightly coiled up, but if you uncoiled them they would take you all the way to the distant planet Pluto and back *six times*. That's the kind of fact that led the psalmist (who didn't know that precise bit of biochemistry) to affirm, 'I am fearfully and wonderfully made' (Ps. 139.14).

Not long ago a spacecraft shot past Pluto. It had taken nine and a half years to get there, travelling the distance of three billion miles at 31,000 miles an hour. It sent back to Earth some remarkable pictures that raced towards us at the speed of light (186,000 miles per second), but even at that speed they took over four hours to arrive. Just to get a handle on the speed of light, think of something travelling around the equator seven and a half times in a second. These are the kind of figures that leave me baffled and amazed. I'm awestruck by their immensity and gaze with even greater wonder and reverence at the night sky. But at least this experience denies me the casual mistake of thinking of spirituality as fluffy personal therapy. If spirituality is concerned with 'eternal truth and love', as Rowan Williams suggests, then these truths are both gritty and vast. I need to enlarge my vision to encompass the wonder of contemporary cosmology.

That's the macro end of wonder. At the micro end is the wonder that comes from encountering the detail of creation. As technology opens to us the ever deeper secrets of the quantum world, we see intricacy and elegance of breathtaking complexity. The thickness of a human hair is equivalent to one million atoms lined up side by side. The nucleus of an atom is, in scale, like a grain of rice in the middle of Wembley Stadium. Bizarrely, an atom is 99.9 per cent empty space so Wembley Stadium, like any other material object, is made up of particles in motion, bouncing around at unimaginable speeds, coming in and out of position billions of times in billionths of a second. It's all truly mind-boggling.

In her own age, it was this experience of wonder that prompted Mother Julian of Norwich, a thirteenth-century 'anchoress', to respond to a simple hazelnut like this:

In this vision he showed me a little thing, the size of a hazelnut, and it was round as a ball. I looked at it with the eye of my understanding and thought 'What may this be?' And it was generally answered thus: 'It is all that is made.' I marvelled how it might last, for it seemed it might suddenly have sunk into nothing because of its littleness. And I was answered in my understanding: 'It lasts and ever shall, because God loves it.' In this little thing I saw three properties. The first is that God made it. The second that God loves it. And the third, that God keeps it.[8]

Here the connection is fully made between the marvel of a tiny scrap of nature's extravagance, and the divine source of all existence. Of course that connection is disputed; no proof is available. But the hypothesis is one that has satisfied and fed millions of people for thousands of years.

Theologians have long spoken of God's two books – the book of Scripture and the book of nature. I think it would be true to say that when I have found the flame of faith growing dim it has been the amazement offered by nature that has most often re-lit the flame. When I walk the hills and mountains I know what the poet meant when she wrote, 'earth's crammed with heaven, and every common bush afire with God'.[9] It's not merely an *adequate* explanation that I look for but a *sufficient* one. Scientific materialism is wonderful at giving adequate answers, but an answer sufficient to carry the full weight of glory on these occasions needs another language as well. The actress Jane Fonda was asked why she had become a Christian, and she said she had been drawn to faith because 'I could feel reverence humming in me.'[10] Very many people experience that reverence before the beauty, the complexity and the power of the living world around us. I'm one of them; maybe you are too?

Key question

Who put the wonder into wonderful?

Story

Slowly, but with no doubt or hesitation whatever, and in something of a solemn expectancy, Rat and Mole passed through
the broken tumultuous water and moored their boat at the
flowery margin of the island. In silence they landed, and pushed
through the blossom and scented herbage and undergrowth
that led up to the level ground, till they stood on a little lawn
of marvellous green, set around with Nature's own orchard
trees – crab apple, wild cherry, and sloe.

'This is the place of my song-dream, the place the music
played to me,' whispered the Rat, as if in a trance. 'Here, in this
holy place, here if anywhere, surely we shall find Him!'

Then suddenly the Mole felt a great Awe fall upon him, an
awe that turned his muscles to water, bowed his head, and
rooted his feet to the ground. It was no panic terror – indeed he
felt wonderfully at peace and happy – but it was an awe that
smote him, and without seeing, he knew it could only mean that
some august Presence was very, very near. With difficulty he
turned to look for his friend and saw him at his side cowed,
stricken, and trembling violently. And still there was utter silence
in the populous bird-haunted branches around them and still
the light grew and grew.

'Rat!' he found breath to whisper, shaking. 'Are you
afraid?'

'Afraid?' murmured the Rat, his eyes shining and with unutterable love. 'Afraid! Of Him? O, never, never! And yet – and
yet – O, Mole, I am afraid!'

Then the two animals, crouching to the earth, bowed their
heads and did worship.

Kenneth Grahame, *The Wind in the Willows*[11]

Poem: Pied Beauty

Glory be to God for dappled things –
For skies of couple-colour as a brinded cow;

For rose-moles all in stipple upon trout that swim;
Fresh-firecoal chestnut-falls; finches' wings;
Landscape plotted and pieced – fold, fallow and plough;
And all trades, their gear and tackle and trim.

All things counter, original, spare, strange;
Whatever is fickle, freckled (who knows how?)
With swift, slow; sweet, sour; adazzle, dim;
He fathers-forth whose beauty is past change;
Praise him.   Gerard Manley Hopkins[12]

Taking it further

If any of this resonates with you, you might like to try some of the following:

1 Think back to moments of amazement that you've experi-enced in the natural world and re-inhabit them for a while. Don't rush. What was it like? What was going on? Ponder the meaning of such 'epiphanies'.
2 Go for a walk in the countryside or the park, and use your senses to enjoy everything around you. (If walking is unrealistic, your own garden could do just as well.) Walk more slowly than usual and notice the distinctiveness of the trees, the subtleties of colour before you, the sensation of the ground beneath your feet, the smells on the air and the caress of wind on your face. All this is gift. Let your spirit respond.
3 If you can, find a square metre of ground or, best of all, a square metre by some water's edge. Be very attentive to that square metre for 15 minutes. Notice everything there, the shape, colour, texture, arrangement of everything, maybe the activity of ants and insects. Let your attentiveness grow into reverence for this complex bit of creation – and the Creator behind it. Stay with it even when you're tempted to walk away.

4 Read chapters 38 and 39 of the Old Testament book of Job. Job has lost everything and has been badly served by his 'comforters', who want him to admit to the wrongdoing that has brought all this ill-fortune upon him. Job protests his innocence and complains to God, but in these last chapters God reminds Job that he is the Creator of the world's wonders. This isn't an answer to the problem of suffering but the chapters serve as a useful primer on God as the Creator of the infinite variety and richness of nature. 'Were you there when I laid the foundations of the earth?' (Answer: no, so perhaps humility and gratitude are appropriate responses.)

6

'Nobody's perfect'

The mess we find ourselves in

———◆•◆•◆———

'Everything feels so messy; I don't know how to sort it out.'

'I wish I could start all over again.'

'Nobody's perfect, but I'm in deep s***.'

* * *

A translation company launched a 'Think Before You Ink' campaign to highlight the risk of botched tattoos. Veritas Language Solutions cited the example of a man who had 'Jenius' tattooed on his forehead; another who asked for the Mandarin symbol for 'live and let live' but instead got the one for 'sweet and sour chicken'; and a woman who used a website to translate 'I love David' into Hebrew and ended up with a tattoo saying: 'Babylon is the world's leading dictionary and translation software.' This seems, in a way, to sum up the predicament that most of us get into: we have the best of intentions, but often get the worst of results.

Have you ever felt that life is somewhat, well, messy? If so, join the club with most of the seven billion other people on the planet. We have a job to do at work. It's complicated, certainly, but it's possible. Why then does it end up all over the place, with the boss muttering something about Mr Bean? A relationship starts out full of promise; days full of beauty and a golden future ahead. Why then is it all falling apart in a firestorm of recriminations? Why has my ideal of happy families with my children descended into a series of High Noon standoffs? Why do I never seem to be able to finish anything? Why does the money never last? Why does life feel like a flat tyre? What's going on – is failure my preferred style?

We wake up in the morning and think, 'How did it come to this?' We had such high hopes for an uncluttered, fulfilling life. Instead, it's a complicated, murky series of evasions and compromises with more frayed edges than straight lines. What went wrong? OK, that optimism was a kind of primal innocence, but was that so bad an aspiration?

My wife is a zealous maker of lists as a way of coping with life's complexities. Indeed, she thinks there are only two types of people in this life – those who make lists, and wimps. So why do I find that when I make lists I write on them things I've already done, just so I can tick them off? Probably because my life feels vaguely out of control and I want to feel I've achieved just something of what I'd set out to do today.

The mess we find ourselves in as we fumble around is often one we initially hope we can manage. Chummy, the midwife and new mother played by Miranda Hart in TV's *Call the Midwife*, says plaintively, 'One feels one should be able to manage.' We do, but chaos still creeps in under the door. And somehow we know that a sympathetic self-help strategy and a breezy time-management course are only going to make us feel worse.

A pilot was once out on a routine flight in bad weather. The pilot turned the controls into a steep ascent and flew straight into the ground. Why? Because the plane had been flying upside down. Sometimes it feels as if the radical nature of our predicament is rather like that. We're flying upside down; one wrong turn and there's no way back. Indeed that feeling of 'no way back' is a depressing bass-note to many lives. But you can't get the toothpaste back in the tube. What's done is done and part of the ongoing messiness of our lives. We lurch into middle age laden with cares and responsibilities, leaving behind us a road strewn with unfilled potholes and memories of dreams that never flew.

Some of this mess is self-induced, a Do It Yourself job. Francis Spufford calls it, delightfully, the Human Propensity to F***

Things Up, or HPtFtU.[1] We are, perhaps, fundamentally addicted to ourselves and to our own pleasure, whatever the cost. The addictions may take obvious forms, like obsessions with wealth, power, sexual adventure, gambling, 'artificial stimulants', visible success. We live in a culture of consumption that promotes these addictions, but also hides them behind the high walls of privacy and individual autonomy. We don't mind the moral cost as long as we can get away with it. But when we fly close to the sun, our wings easily get burned and we crash into the ground morally, spiritually or in some other more obvious way. There are dark, unmanageable continents of the human heart that provide good evidence for what we may not want to call 'sin' but which nevertheless leave our lives shattered. Alexander Solzhenitsyn said, 'The line separating good and evil passes not through states, not between classes, not between political parties, but through every human heart.' HPtFtU.

Throughout my adult years I've sometimes been accused of compartmentalizing the different elements of my life and the people in it. I've been told that I'm over-concerned with keeping things neat and in order. In response I've tried to explain that this has been a panic-based strategy to stay sane. I've usually been paddling furiously under water to stay afloat. In order not to be overwhelmed with what I've taken on, what I couldn't avoid, and my own insecurities, I've devised defensive schemes to keep me off medication. The appearance of a calm and orderly life has been like keeping visitors in a tidy living room while the kitchen is a disaster area.

What, then, shall we do with this mess, or with the dis-ease we feel when we listen to our heart?

What most of us experience, to some degree, at certain stages of our lives is only one expression of a deeper messiness in life as a whole. 'There's a crack in everything,' sang Leonard Cohen.[2] It's the mess of a broken heart, a broken life or a broken nation. It's the darkness that flies on the wind and then descends in communal hatreds, random killings, and rape as a weapon of war. It's the terror of a cancer diagnosis, the horror of an earthquake or the outrageous death of a child. We have the experience of being unstrung, and as we observe our world it feels that the whole of life reeks of danger. Every time we watch the news we're regaled with evidence of the large-scale messiness of life, whether it be the unimaginable brutality of ISIS, the insistent warnings of climate catastrophe, the seemingly irresistible demand for war, the human misery of refugees and mass migration, the threat of biological, cyber or nuclear terrorism, and much else besides. There is indeed a crack in everything.

But 'that's how the light gets in', continues Leonard Cohen. Our experience of mess, whether personally or globally, can lead us to look more urgently for sources of light and hope. Martin Luther King once said, 'Darkness cannot cast out darkness; only light can do that. Hate cannot cast out hate, only love can do that.'[3] Perhaps we begin to realize, again either personally or globally, that we missed something back at the pass. Love is an absolute value that we mustn't debase, distort or dilute. To do so is to be in danger of losing our way in a world where everything is relative and nothing has real value. That way we end up flying upside down.

W. H. Auden was once sitting in a Manhattan cinema watching the horrors that the Nazis had perpetrated on the Jews. His belief in the goodness of humanity suddenly collided with the evidence of appalling evil flashing before him. He concluded, 'If I was to say *that* was evil, I had to have a standard by which to do so. I didn't have one. I'd spent all my adult life as an intellectual destroying the absolutes, and now suddenly I needed one to be able to say that this was wrong.'[4] He left the cinema in search of some absolutes and soon made his way to faith.

Perhaps we've got so used to looking in distorted mirrors that we can't see true images very easily. We end up with no straight lines, only various degrees of curve. But eventually we find we can't live with total relativism, without any moral plumb lines. We need sane measures for our lives and some prospect of order. Where are these to come from if we live in a closed system, a world without reference beyond itself?

George Orwell, a noted atheist, was coming towards the end of his life and reflecting on the loss of religious faith in Europe, a process he had once much applauded but which now dismayed him:

> For two hundred years we have sawed and sawed at the branch we were sitting on. And in the end, much more suddenly than we had foreseen, our efforts were rewarded and down we came. But unfortunately there had been a little mistake. The thing at the bottom was not a bed of roses after all; it was a cesspool of barbed wire . . . It appears that amputation of the soul is not a simple surgical job, like having your appendix out. The wound has a tendency to go septic.[5]

Our experience of the messiness of life may therefore – rather unexpectedly – open up channels of hope as we realize we have to look deeper if we're to make sense of things. It may seem obvious, but if we feel helpless, we need help; if we feel lost, we need directions; if we feel all at sea, we need dry land; if we feel destabilized we need a still centre. Our catastrophes could persuade us that there is simply nowhere else to go but to the patient love of a greater Reality. The mess I keep hidden through my 'compartmentalization' strategy could eventually encourage me to seek help in sorting it out. If the great spiritual teachers are to be believed there is a Love which never lets you down and never lets you go.

Yes, there's a crack in everything, but that's how the light gets in.

Key question

Are we mentally and spiritually flying upside down? How might we turn ourselves the right way up?

Poem

A haiku appeared outside a street café, entitled 'Haiku for getting up in the morning'. It went:

No, No, No, No, No
No, No, No, No, No, No, No
No, No, No, No, No

To think about

If you live with the devil you find out there is a God.
                                                    Sinead O'Connor[6]

We are all in the gutter, but some of us are looking at the stars.   Oscar Wilde[7]

Taking it further

If it's helpful, here are some ideas to try out:

1 When life is a mess one of the first things to do may be to break the mess down into smaller pieces, which hopefully makes them more manageable. It may therefore be helpful to divide the problems into two lists, one headed 'My responsibility', the other 'Not my fault'. Now at least you know what you could address personally.

2 Do you need outside help to handle these issues, wherever they came from? Presuming most of us do gain benefit from such help, this person may be a counsellor, a life-coach, a priest, or a friend to talk to over a drink. The greatest problem is overcoming our reticence and pride: 'One feels one should be able to manage.' Break through that barrier and deep, realistic help is nearly always available.

3 Sometimes the mess we're in is mainly our own fault, in which case some way of dispersing the guilt is extremely valuable. The secular route is usually through counselling.

The alternative spiritual route is traditionally called confession and can either be arranged personally with a priest, or undertaken seriously in private before God. In either case it's helpful to write out the things you are getting rid of in this way – that piece of paper can be ritually burned afterwards.

4 Read Henri Nouwen's book *The Return of the Prodigal Son* (Darton, Longman and Todd, 1994). This classic meditation on Rembrandt's painting of the same name reflects on the themes of homecoming, affirmation and reconciliation and opens up compelling vistas of hope, wherever we feel we are in the story.

7

'Hell and high water'

The poignant questions of suffering

'It hurts so much it feels more than I can carry.'

'No one could ever understand what I'm going through.'

'Life will never be the same again.'

* * *

As I write I have on my desk a piece of paper on which are a few sentences written by a young boy in Uganda, given to me by my daughter after her gap year there. She had asked the children to write about the best and worst days of their lives and young Patrick wrote this:

> The best of my life was when I am in Kampala. In fact the day it was good because I found a European man in the Sheraton Hotel and he asked that do you like football and I answered him that I liked so much. Within two minutes he gave me a football. That's my best day on my life now. The worst day on my life was the day when my father was died and my mother became a mad woman. I was five years old when he died.

The poignancy of that piece of writing cuts through me every time I read it.

In the firestorm of life everyone gets burned, but we don't know when and from what source the blistering flames will arrive. It doesn't help particularly to know of the deepest wounds that happen to other people, ours are enough; nevertheless we tend to measure ourselves against these extremes and wonder how we would cope. In the single month of March 1856 Archibald Tait, then Dean of Carlisle and later Archbishop of Canterbury, lost five of his daughters to scarlet fever. The silent nursery must have been a terrible test of his faith and that of his wife. Just yesterday I read of a 43-year-old man who had a heart attack and died in his bathroom; as he collapsed he fell on to his one-year-old son and suffocated him. How do parents survive these things? How do they remain sane?

And of course the cry of grief is a standing protest against belief in any concept of a loving God. Some situations are simply dripping with darkness. Elie Wiesel was a teenager in Auschwitz and after watching a child hanged before the eyes of the whole camp, he wrote, 'I shall never forget the moments which murdered my God and my soul. I shall never forget the flames which consumed my faith forever.' And yet, reflecting on the whole horror of the story he concluded, 'We cannot understand it with God. And we cannot understand without him.'[1]

Actor and writer Stephen Fry felt no such ambivalence when he was being interviewed on Irish television about what he would say to God if he met him. His tirade is magnificent in its totality.

> I'll say, bone cancer in children, what's that about? How dare you? How dare you create a world in which there is such misery that is not our fault? It's not right, it's utterly, utterly evil. Why should I respect a capricious, mean-minded, stupid God who creates a world that is so full of injustice and pain? ... The god who created this universe, if it was created by god, is quite clearly a maniac, utter maniac, totally selfish. We have to spend our lives on our knees thanking him? ... It's perfectly apparent he's monstrous, utterly monstrous, and deserves no respect whatsoever.[2]

And yet, practically all the major religions have grown out of the intractable experience of suffering. Judaism had its foundational events in the exodus from Egypt and the exile in Babylon, both involving captivity and dark years. Christianity has at its heart a man undergoing immense suffering and death on behalf of others. Islam's founder, Muhammad, was a soldier who knew the price of warfare. Buddhism arose out of the Buddha's concern to solve the riddle of suffering, the answer to which he found in the ability to overcome desire. Most religions are entwined around the tree of human suffering. Indeed those sects that aren't seriously engaged with the wounds of humanity are in danger of falling into the trap of self-help therapies. The universality of suffering makes it the Great Pretender that undermines the joy of life, and it's therefore inevitably the experience that we seek to understand and cope with in our most profound reflections on life, which is the stuff of spirituality and religion.

Put simply, there are three different issues which are likely to be prominent in our experience of suffering – the need to cope with it emotionally, the desire to face it spiritually, and the call to understand it intellectually. The *emotional response* is uniquely mysterious; each person makes his or her own way through the labyrinthine paths of pain and grief, burrowing deep underground and emerging only occasionally for supplies. Loved ones can only keep vigil, listen attentively, and pass supplies down into the pit. The best help usually comes from those who remain present and keep silent. Words so easily offend with their inadequacy and cheap solutions. The nerve ends of our emotions heal slowly in their own silence and space.

The *spiritual response* we make is equally mysterious and, at first, will probably be shaped by past experience. It's unlikely, for example, that Stephen Fry would be calling on the resources of religion and its witness to the inexhaustible love of God. But this is where surprising discoveries are made by many sufferers. Because trivia are stripped away, the crucial issues of life and death, love and loss, forgiveness and compassion are exposed as never before. Ultimate questions can't be ducked any longer; at last we have to be serious.

Barbara Brown Taylor puts it like this. 'Pain makes theologians of us all. When pain is as ubiquitous as air, why comment on it? Better to go where the pain leads, down to the ground floor where all the real things are: real love, real sorrow, real thanks, real fear. After a tête-à-tête down there, you can lose your appetite for tabloid gossip and shopping news.'[3]

You can also lose what faith you had. Suffering like this, our own or that of people close to us, is often the great watershed for belief in a divine presence at the heart of things. It's before and after, yes or no, sense or nonsense. For some people, their desperate prayers seem to be met by the deafening silence of an empty universe, and the shutters finally come down on belief in God. For others, the sharpness and ultimacy of the experience breaks open the concrete that may have set over these faith issues, and spiritual questions begin to leak in. Questions don't necessarily lead to answers, but they do lead to an important struggle to make sense of life's complexity.

One of the most common experiences in significant illness is that a yawning distance opens up between the all-consuming seriousness of the person who's engaged in that silent struggle, and the rest of the world getting on with life as if everything is the same, and all that matters is what's happening in Coronation Street and the latest gossip on Twitter. No; everything has changed and many of us are looking for spiritual resources equal to the task of interpretation, survival, memory, hope, love and meaning.

The Christian story then points to the cross, that silent source of empathy to which millions have turned in various states of belief and doubt and been met by a Love beyond description. Many a time I have given someone trudging through the dark valley of suffering a small cross to hang on to. The cross is not in that case looking for an argument or even offering an answer; it's there as an embrace, an understanding, a deep, rueful smile, and a source of unlimited compassion.

St Teresa said of suffering, 'You do not fall out of the hands of God; you fall into them.'

There is, then, a need to cope with suffering emotionally and, quite possibly, a desire to face it spiritually. Third, there may be an *intellectual response*, a need to understand the experience, though this may arise much later on when the crisis has passed. If God is love, why should all this happen? Why couldn't the Cosmic Plumber fix it? Of course, if we think a little longer about the nature of love we realize that it can only really exist between free beings. It can't be demanded, bought or forced. Love lets go. Love does all that love can do, but any loving God worthy of the name would limit his/her absolute power in the interests of love, just as a parent restricts his or her absolutist tendencies in the very act of creating an independent being.

Freedom comes at a price. It's woven into the fabric of creation; it's not detachable so that parts (love, compassion, courage) are given and other parts (earthquakes, cancer, wars) are withheld. Freedom is as seamless as love, and as vulnerable. It has a price, that of accidents and cells that go wrong and tectonic plates that move.

Ultimately we have to accept that suffering isn't a problem to explain; it's a mystery to enter, with others. It needs not explanation but participation.

That profound experience of participation is movingly exemplified by Etty Hillesum, a 28-year-old Dutch Jew who discovered, during the Second World War, an extraordinary capacity to unify the joy of life and the horror of a concentration camp. Only latterly had she found faith through literature, philosophy and an unusual psychotherapist, but she brought a hugely mature spirit to the unspeakable events around her.

> The misery here is quite terrible; and yet, late at night when the day has slunk away into the depths behind me, I often walk with a spring in my step along the barbed wire. And then time and again it soars straight from my

heart – I can't help it, that's just the way it is, like some elementary force – the feeling that life is glorious and magnificent, and that one day we shall be building a whole new world. Against every new outrage and every fresh horror we shall put up one more piece of love and goodness, drawing strength from within ourselves. We may suffer, but we must not succumb.[4]

A few months before she died she wrote, 'If I knew for certain that I should die next week, I should still be able to sit at my desk and study with perfect equanimity, for I know now that life and death make a meaningful whole . . . Death is slipping away, even when gloom and abominations are its trappings.' Or again, 'The realms of the soul and the spirit are so spacious and unending that this little bit of physical discomfort doesn't matter all that much. I do not feel I have been robbed of my freedom; essentially no one can do me any harm at all . . .'[5]

Here emotional freedom, spiritual equanimity and intellectual inquisitiveness have coalesced into a profound ability to look clearly into the truth that faced her and not be afraid.

The experience of suffering drives straight to the heart of the spiritual search that this book is about. By its very uncompromising 'in your face' boorishness, suffering demands a serious response. It could be a doorway into the surprising treasures of darkness.

Key question

Is suffering the death knell for belief in God, or is there a door that beckons beyond?

To think about

The world breaks everyone, and afterwards many are strong in the broken places. Ernest Hemingway

To love at all is to be vulnerable. Love anything, and your heart will certainly be wrung and possibly be broken. If you want to make sure of keeping it intact, you must give your heart to no one, not even to an animal. Wrap it carefully around with hobbies and little luxuries; avoid all entanglements; lock it up safely in the casket or coffin of your selfishness. But in that casket – safe, dark, motionless, airless – it will change. It will not be broken; it will become unbreakable, impenetrable, irredeemable. The alternative to tragedy, or at least to the risk of tragedy, is damnation. The only place outside Heaven where you can be perfectly safe from all dangers and perturbations of love is Hell.   C. S. Lewis[6]

'There cannot be a God of love,' they say, 'because if there was and he looked upon the world, his heart would break.' The Church points to the cross and says, 'It did break.' 'It's God who made the world,' they say. 'It's he who should bear the load.' The Church points to the cross and says, 'He did bear it.'   William Temple[7]

God did not say 'You will not be troubled, you will not be belaboured, you will not be disquieted,' but he said 'You will not be overcome.'   Mother Julian of Norwich[8]

Taking it further

1 Carry a stone in your pocket. Hold it when necessary and try to discharge the dark electricity of your suffering, or the suffering of another, into that hard stone. As a variation, carry a small cross.

2 Who can you trust with your suffering? That is, who would listen carefully, stay with you and say little, but be wise? Sometimes an unexpected name emerges when you ask that question, and that's the person to ask to listen to you for a while. Use the conversation to think about two questions:

(1) What do you want to do with this suffering? (Jesus said to a blind man, 'What do you want me to do for you?' Obvious, you'd have thought, but Jesus knew there was a cost to being healed, such as loss of the status of being 'blind' or loss of earnings through almsgiving.) (2) What help do you need?

3 Read Luke 22 and 23. Encounter the cross, and when you've imbibed that dark grace, move on to chapter 24.

4 If you want to pursue the intellectual issue of a good God and a suffering world, a helpful, if demanding, place to start is with John V. Taylor in his book *The Christlike God* (London: SCM, 1992), chapters 7 and 8. He says elsewhere, 'The truth about God is not so much that he is omnipotent as that he is inexhaustible, and for that reason he cannot fail.' Does that make sense to you?

8

'Don't just do something, sit there'
A need for stillness

—————◆•●•◆—————

'I desperately need more stillness in my life.'

'I never realized how much I would value being silent.'

'Why doesn't life obey the speed limit?'

* * *

The question was asked in an Oxford history paper, 'Was Queen Mary a good queen? Be brief.' One candidate wrote 'Yes'. The examiner wrote in the margin, 'A good, brief answer. But a better, and briefer, one would have been "No".'

Society is deeply in need of brief answers. We're overwhelmed with words. They pour over us from the moment we wake up and turn on the radio. We're saturated in them all day, whether they come at us in newsprint, email, texts, Twitter, Snapchat, Facebook, WhatsApp, the internet, television, or even those extraordinary old survivors, letters and books. By the end of the day we can feel battered by the words of others, and promiscuous in our own use of them. Something deep inside many of us cries out for another language – the language of silence.

It's not as if most of the words we use are particularly effective. Barbara Brown Taylor writes, 'Most of the words offered to us have been chewed so many times there are no nutrients left in them, or else they have been left uncovered on some shelf until they are too hard to bite into.'[1] Words are precious. They're gifts to be used carefully to communicate information, meaning, truth and love. Words are supple, fluent, fragile – but they can also be degraded and used as weapons, harsh, biting, brutal. They're wonderful and dangerous, beautiful and terrible. But above all, there are too many of them.

As one who has been to more church services than is reasonable to expect of any individual of sound mind and body, I'm often dismayed at how little space or silence there is in them. If someone offers me a moment of silence in a service, I dive into it like a dehydrated pilgrim finding a well in the desert. What I need isn't more words to stimulate me; I need more space to allow a few significant words to settle deep within me and feed me with wisdom. It's like a glass of dirty water from a pond. When it's agitated, the dirt swirls around and remains unpleasantly visible. But when the glass is allowed to be still, the dirt begins to separate and drift to the bottom of the glass, leaving the water above clear and inviting. The same thing can happen to our clouded, bewildered souls; they need space to settle and separate out, and for our dreams to clarify and open to the light.

Not only words, but time too, is under sustained pressure in contemporary society. Human ingenuity has produced time-saving technologies of all kinds, and yet somehow we have less time than ever before. As a society we have our foot hard on the accelerator so that we have more time to enjoy our leisure, but simultaneously we've invented new forms of communication which eat up our spare time faster than we can save it. Life should get a speeding ticket, or at least go on a speed awareness course. I remember being thrilled when email emerged and I could deal with minor matters so quickly; I was less thrilled when emails began to besiege me, overwhelm me, and finally take me captive. There's more to life than an empty inbox.

Most of us long for a more spacious life. We define it in different ways, but we know instinctively that there's a healthier way of arranging our priorities and deploying our energies, and it's something to do with stillness and silence. The Orthodox

Bishop Kallistos Ware puts it rather more dramatically. 'Unless there is a centre in the middle of a storm; unless a man [sic] in the midst of all his activities preserves a secret room in his heart where he stands alone before God, he will lose all sense of spiritual direction and be torn to pieces.'[2] That last phrase is particularly vivid, but we are probably more vulnerable than we think to the wilder beasts of the contemporary forest, and most of us probably need to find that inner space whereby we can keep quiet counsel and connect with our spiritual heartbeat.

Somewhere, not far under the surface, most of us already know we need that space and stillness. Retreat centres proliferate. Television programmes on monastic life are viewed ravenously. Tens of thousands of 'maybe' pilgrims walk the well-worn path to Santiago de Compostela. In major bookshops shelves labelled 'Mind, Body, Spirit' dwarf those of religion. Sunday colour supplements regularly offer articles on how to downsize, drop out or quieten down. Prayers for stressed commuters appear on the London Underground. Mindfulness has swept through the country in courses, books and dinner-party conversations. Some schools have introduced mindfulness as a core practice, little realizing that it's rooted as much in Christian contemplative prayer as in Buddhist meditation (although in its contemporary manifestation its pedigree is essentially eastern). The academic behind the recent resurgence of mindfulness in the UK, Mark Williams, is not only Emeritus Professor of Clinical Psychology at Oxford University but also an ordained Honorary Canon of Christ Church Cathedral. Wherever you look, just under the frenetic surface of twenty-first-century life, there's a deep thirst for stillness.

I was encouraged when I realized that the words 'silent' and 'listen' are made up of the same letters. Silence isn't made up of a desperate determination to shut out all noise, both inside and outside ourselves, so that we can be free of distractions and hear the pure voice of God feeding us words of inspiration

56

and peace. If we only look for that rare and special experience the more likely result will be failure and disillusion. Silence is a quiet, patient listening that doesn't struggle with distractions but looks over their shoulder. It doesn't become anxious when nothing is heard, but keeps returning to a chosen key word or phrase that anchors the heart. Silence isn't looking for results, feelings and words of honey; through it, though, we offer ourselves to God, the Absolute, or whatever shape we give to the spiritual core of life. Stillness gives us the space to absorb rather than to process, to receive rather than to analyse. The heart of it is the 'being there', and the hardest task of all is turning away from our obsession with ourselves in order to stay with the moment and attend to the Other.

When our minds are full of the social-media chatter of present-day existence, listening is a particularly counter-intuitive disposition. We're used to being the centre of the chatter and keeping the people around us entertained with our wit and wisdom. But a good listener is a gift from God. Anyone wounded in the front line of life will witness to the redemptive value of that listening. Similarly, listening is the heart of the practice of stillness. A journalist interviewed Mother Teresa about her prayer life. 'What words do you use when you pray to God?' he asked. Mother Teresa replied, 'I don't speak much to God; I just listen to him.' 'What does God say?' asked the journalist, intrigued. 'He just listens too,' said Mother Teresa.

The value of silence and contemplative prayer can come as a sweet surprise. Some medical students enrolled on a module on Spirituality and Healthcare at Brighton and Sussex Medical School and received some basic 'spiritual skills training'. One said later, 'It really is amazing how connected a person can feel when they restrict their conscious thought. Shortly after starting, I started to feel the breeze and hear the sounds coming in through the window. I sensed the light warming the room, and almost felt light-headed from what I can only describe as the *richness* of what I was perceiving.'[3] Another spiritually aware person suggested something similar: 'If you sit very still, you can hear the sun move.'

There's a vast interior wilderness in each of us and in many cases it has barely been explored. When we stumble into it, the experience can be transformative. Young people naturally have their heads full of instant messaging, homework, iTunes, romantic fantasy, Xbox, sports teams, exams, unreasonable parents, weekend parties, doubtful substances, school rivalries, etc., so it's often a considerable surprise to find this mysterious 'in-scape' where nothing is quite as it seems, everything is richer and deeper than they'd imagined, and no one has given them a map for the exploration. Of course, it's not just young people who make this discovery; it's just that young people are more open to fundamental life choices based on new experiences. But whatever your age, this is adventure like no other, tackling great things.

The Austrian Baron von Hügel knew about these 'great things' and in a letter to his niece he wrote, 'Be silent about great things, let them grow inside you. Never discuss them: discussion is so limiting and distracting. It makes things grow smaller. You think you swallow things when they ought to swallow you. Before all greatness, be silent – in art, in music, in religion: silence.'[4] The wilderness and silence of our inner lives, where the 'great things' lie, are hard to mention to others for fear of misunderstanding and ridicule. But they are present in every life. They are the birthplace of prayer and – some of us believe – the dwelling place of God. As Meister Eckhart said centuries ago, 'Nothing in all creation is so like God as stillness.'

Key question

Do we dare slow down and explore our inner space, knowing it could both release the peace we desire, and also expose the unresolved issues we might have buried?

Story

Sarapion the Sindonite went on pilgrimage to Rome. He was told of a famous recluse who lived there, very simply, in one room. As a great traveller who couldn't imagine such inactivity Sarapion was sceptical about this, so he called on the recluse and asked her, 'Why do you just sit here?' She replied, 'I'm not sitting. I'm on a journey.'

Poem: Kneeling

Moments of great calm
Kneeling before an altar
Of wood in a stone church
In summer, waiting for God
To speak; the air a staircase
For silence; the sun's light
Ringing me, as though I acted
A great role. And the audience
Still; all that close throng
Of spirits waiting, as I,
For the message.
                    Prompt me, God
But not yet. When I speak
Though it be you who speak
Through me, something is lost.
The meaning is in the waiting.
                    R. S. Thomas[5]

Taking it further

If this resonates with you, you might like to try some of the following:

1 Experiment with silence. Don't take on too much too soon, just start with five minutes, then ten; let it grow naturally. Settle into a place where you can be both comfortable and alert. Be aware of the tension in parts of your body – typically the

shoulders and around the eyes – and then consciously relax them. Be aware of the noises from outside, identify them and let them go. Do the same with the noises and chatter inside you; identify them and let them go. Then take a word or phrase and use it as the 'centring word' which you repeat when necessary to bring your mind back from its inevitable wanderings. I use words like 'Before you, Lord', 'Come, Holy Spirit', or simply 'Jesus'. You might prefer words that are less overtly Christian: 'Be still', 'Peace', or simply 'Yes'. Don't expect a holy glow or even a particular experience or awareness; just offer yourself to God (as you understand 'God') and let God be present. You might walk away and wonder what that was all about, and that's fine; I don't remember most of the evening meals I've had in my life, but I know I would be infinitely the poorer without them. Be sure, something valuable will have gone on in that period of silence, some touch, some clearing of the water in the glass, some alchemy of the Spirit. Some people find it helpful to light a candle to mark out this special time, and to have a notepad available to jot down the random, but important, thoughts that pop up in your mind from time to time.

2 Take the phrase from Psalm 46, 'Be still, and know that I am God.' Repeat the phrase slowly and carefully; savour it, soak yourself in it. Then let the last word drop off so that you say simply, 'Be still, and know that I am.' Taste the freshness of that phrase. Enjoy the silence and simplicity of the moment. Take time. Then, again, drop off the last words, leaving 'Be still, and know.' Savour the words and the meaning. Then reduce the phrase to 'Be still.' Don't be hurried. Finally reduce the phrase to its core, 'Be . . .'. Eventually, you could build back up in the opposite direction, or equally, wait, and be lightly touched by love.

3 Recognize that you might be tiptoeing into the territory of prayer, and that may draw out other responses. We have many instincts that come naturally to us every day – *gratitude*

for a kindness or the colours of the sky, *sorrow* for the mess we've made in a particular relationship or through a bad decision, the *needs of others* that touch our hearts, viewed on the news or seen in the street. All these instincts – gratitude, sorrow, need – are the birthplace of prayer because it isn't an extravagant step to direct these familiar instincts towards God, and to stretch them out as desired. Prayer keeps leaking out of us, even if, inconveniently, we don't believe in God.

4 Read Sara Maitland's *A Book of Silence* (London: Granta, 2008) in which she describes how, in her late forties and after many noisy years as a vocal feminist and mother, she found herself falling in love with silence. It's fascinating, intelligent and witty. Other books on the wider subject of prayer could be (with apologies) my *How to Pray* (London: SPCK, 2002), which contains a wide range of suggestions for different ways of praying, or David Wilkinson's *When I Pray, What Does God Do?* (Oxford: Monarch, 2015), where an ordained scientist explores the question in the title.

A final story

If we're getting into the wider arena of prayer, here's one person's starting point. Elizabeth Gilbert was on a one-year 'search for everything' that took her around the world. Her story begins with the breakdown of her marriage and an incident when she's on the bathroom floor in the middle of the night and feeling desperate, so much so that's she's ready to pray, but not sure how.

'Hello, God. How are you? I'm Liz. It's nice to meet you.'

That's right, I was speaking to the creator of the universe as though we'd just been introduced at a cocktail party. In fact it was all I could do to stop myself saying, 'I've always been a big fan of your work . . .'

'I'm sorry to bother you so late at night, but I'm in serious trouble. And I'm sorry I haven't ever spoken to you directly before. I'm not an expert at praying, as you know. But can you please help me? I am in desperate need of help. I don't know what to do. I need an answer. Please tell me what to do. Please tell me what to do. Please tell me what to do.'

Elizabeth Gilbert, *Eat, Pray, Love*[6]

This was a turning point for Elizabeth Gilbert, not a religious conversion, she says, but the beginning of a religious conversation that brought her very close to God.

9

'Tell it slant'

The disturbing beauty of the arts

———◆•◆•◆———

'I feel a kind of awe in front of great paintings.'

'Music sometimes moves me more deeply than I can say.'

'Why do I get so emotional at a line of poetry?'

* * *

'I can't listen to too much Wagner,' said Woody Allen. 'I start to get the urge to conquer Poland.' There's no doubt that music – and other forms of what we rather lazily call 'the arts' – can have an effect on us that's much more profound than we expect. In a culture of daytime television, celebrity magazines and trivial tweets, the arts enrich our lives with depth and with that elusive 'something more'. We are stirred, elated, comforted, challenged, opened up. Sometimes I'm listening to a piece of great music and I'm thrilled beyond measure; I find myself grinning inanely and, like Herod with his stepdaughter Salome, would give away half my fortune (which luckily isn't much).

When I was in my teens and my parents were away, I was sometimes invited to Sunday lunch by a generous couple who loved music. After the meal we would retire to a room made sacred by the presence of hundreds of vinyl discs and two huge speakers, and there I was inducted into the mysteries of the classics. We would sit as if at a concert, without distraction or interval, and I would be swept into the magisterial presence of Beethoven's symphonies, Brahms' piano concertos and Tchaikovsky's passionate repertoire. Hours later I would leave that ordinary suburban house with my heart full to overflowing. It was the beginning of my musical education and I knew I was on the edge of something vast.

But what, precisely?

Music, art and literature can offer us a reflection of our own lives. We recognize our experiences and the experiences of others, and that can be reassuring or unnerving. We can be more confident that we understand a bit about life's complexities, or we can experience sweet pain that empties us out through poignant memory or the awareness of our mortality. We smile with recognition or wince with regret. Above all, these art forms take us on a journey, most obviously in the case of novels and films but also with music and paintings; we come out of a concert hall or an exhibition and realize we've been somewhere different and special and now we have to return. But how far does that journey go, and in what direction?

It's always interesting to me to note how similarly the experiences of going to church, and going to a great concert or major exhibition, seem to operate. The reverent entry, the hush of expectation, the communal attentiveness, the relaxation at the end as the experience releases you from its imaginative grip. There's no doubt that appreciation of the arts can act as an alternative religion in many lives, and understandably so. But for some people there's still a tantalizing question, a quiet invitation, hanging around unanswered.

Writer and broadcaster Bel Mooney wrote that agnostics like her 'tiptoe towards the deity while listening to music . . . Art has the power to make the universe shiver.'[1] The great cellist Pablo Casals clearly echoed that intuition. He once said:

> For the last eighty years I've started every day in the same way. It's not a mechanical routine but something essential to my daily life. I go to the piano and play two preludes and fugues by Bach. I can't think of doing otherwise. It's a sort of benediction on the house. But that's not its only

meaning for me. It's a rediscovery of the world of which I have the joy of being a part. It fills me with the awareness of the wonder of life, with a feeling of the incredible marvel of being a human being.[2]

The language of other artists teeters on the same brink. Picasso said, 'The great artistic problem is how to get something of the absolute into the frog pond.'[3] Less prosaically, playwright Eve Ensler said:

Theatre has the potential to bring us into a world of ambiguity and paradox, to unlock positional thinking, to shatter taboos, to disrupt the normal patterns of our brain. Art has the capacity to explode the heart and open up other energetic capacities. It defies boundaries and leaps tall buildings. It transports, it translates, it transcends. Transcendence is so important right now because our lives are so mechanized, controlled and commodified; art has the capacity to open our souls and could be our revolutionary, evolutionary salvation.[4]

And this is where some agnostics begin to get uncomfortable. They may feel that their attraction to aesthetics is being hijacked into religious captivity. It's one thing to affirm the remarkable ability of art, music, poetry or theatre to change the way we look at the world; it's acceptable to speak of moments of disclosure, even epiphanies. But when words like 'soul' and 'salvation' start creeping in we're clearly letting our imaginations run away with themselves. Richard Dawkins pulls on the reins. 'Obviously Beethoven's late quartets are sublime. So are Shakespeare's sonnets. They are sublime if God is there and they are sublime if he isn't. They do not prove the existence of God, they prove the existence of Beethoven and Shakespeare.'[5]

We can agree with Dawkins' note of caution but still be fascinated by the significance of this liminal territory where artistic beauty overlaps with spiritual transcendence. There's no way of resolving these two interpretations of what we see, read or hear. On the one hand, the experience of great art could be evidence of God's generous creativity, whereby the patterns of the universe imprint themselves on the minds of sensitive men and women in such a way that they express their consequent delight by creating great art. On the other hand, great art could simply thrill us as sublime expressions of the creativity of sensitive men and women working from the depths of their genius. Such an explanation can be complete in itself; there's no need to add sugar.

I first heard Morten Lauridsen's *O Magnum Mysterium* when Canterbury Cathedral Choir went to Rome to celebrate the 1400th anniversary of Pope Gregory sending Augustine to England in AD 597. They sang that superb piece of music during the Mass in one of Rome's largest churches, and I was transported by its evocative, ethereal beauty. In the context of worship and the church's ancient, prayerful stones I found it utterly compelling in its witness to the glorious mystery of God. A short time later I used a recording of that piece in a meditation for a conference of counsellors that included, inevitably, both believers and non-believers. There were rumblings that the music was inappropriate. In this different context it was asking too much of some of its audience; they felt it was asking them to believe. Music takes us to the door of transcendence but only some will go through and find divinity.

And yet there's this perennial problem of 'the remainder'. It's difficult to stuff the entirety of the artistic experience into the materialist box. It keeps on overflowing. To describe the Bruch violin concerto as the product of horse hair scraping over catgut doesn't feel adequate. There's more to be said. Indeed that word 'more' is a key one in this discussion. The audacious ballet dancer Sylvie Guillem described her art in this way: 'The stage is like a magnifier of thoughts and emotion and vibration; that's what the stage is incredible for, because it makes you live other lives, it makes you experience other emotions, it makes you feel more beautiful, or more alone, or more angry, it makes you feel much *more, more, more*.'[6] There always seems to be 'more' in art; the problem is to name it adequately.

Novelist Jeanette Winterson has another metaphor for this 'more'. She tries the idea of rooms:

> What art communicates, if it's genuine, is something ineffable. Something about ourselves, about the human condition, that is not summed up by the oil painting, or the piece of music, or the poem, but, rather, *moves through it*. What you say, what you paint, what you can hear, is the means not the end of art; there are *so many rooms behind*. [my italics][7]

But what are the name plates on these rooms? How do you explain or describe what they represent? Perhaps Schumann got it right when, after he had played a particularly difficult étude, he was asked by a member of the audience if he would explain it. In reply, Schumann simply sat down and played it again. Explanations belong to the realm of science, engineering, law and economics. Great art is more like a wonderful joke – you try and explain it at your peril.

The bottom line is that 'art and religion always shadow one another', says writer Julian Barnes. They do it 'through the abstract nouns they both invoke: truth, seriousness, imagination, sympathy, morality, transcendence'.[8] No one can claim exclusive rights to this territory, but it's surely worth pursuing the question and seeing which interpretation, materialist or spiritual, makes more sense to us. And if we find that we can't rest content that the music of Bach is just wonderful physics, we might want to try and inhabit the other perception – that when the universe shivers it's because it's echoing the incredible Mystery that underlies it.

Key question

Having got to the doorway of transcendence through the arts, what now?

To think about

Poetry offers a clarification, a fleeting glimpse of a potential order of things beyond confusion.   Seamus Heaney[9]

Today like every other day we wake up empty and frightened. Don't open the door to the study and begin reading. Take down a musical instrument. Let the beauty we love be what we do. There are hundreds of ways to kneel and kiss the ground.   Rumi[10]

> Unless the eye catch fire, the God will not be seen.
> Unless the ear catch fire, the God will not be heard.
> Unless the tongue catch fire, the God will not be
>   named.
> Unless the heart catch fire, the God will not be loved.
> Unless the mind catch fire, the God will not be
>   known.   William Blake[11]

Extract

In the end Hans Küng [the well-known theologian] is forced back to speak of 'the ineffable mystery' that is in the midst of music, adding that for him it is Mozart's music more than any other that reveals how wafer-thin is the boundary between the human and the divine. He claims that, 'to listen to the adagio of the Clarinet Concerto, for example, is to perceive something wholly other: the sound of an infinite which transcends us and for which "beauty" is no description . . . To describe such experience and revelation of transcendence, religious language still needs the word God.' In the end, the artist, the poet, the playwright, the novelist, the composer, in answer to T. S. Eliot's taxi driver's question: 'What's it all about then?' is saying: 'This is what it looks like to me. Let me show you in the most adequate language I know.' And the greatest of them is able, mysteriously and wonderfully, to show us not just the essence of a landscape or the inner workings of the human heart, *but to show us these things under the aspect of eternity* [my italics]. Whether it is Monet finally triumphing over how the light falls on his waterlilies, or Cézanne capturing the elusive subtleties of Mont Saint Victoire, or Shakespeare penetrating into the heart of Lear, each in their own unique way calls attention to how things are: they praise the world 'for being and for happening'. My contention is that, by watching where they plant their steps, we can do the same.

Michael Mayne, *This Sunrise of Wonder*[12]

Taking it further

If this seems like a fruitful avenue to explore, here are some ideas:

1 Listen to one of your favourite pieces of music but this time suspend your disbelief and listen to it as a person of faith. See what it feels like to attribute the beauty of the music to a God of beauty.

2 Read one or both of two enthralling books on Christian paintings and their meanings: Richard Harries, *The Passion in Art* (Aldershot: Ashgate, 2004); John Drury, *Painting the Word* (New Haven: Yale, 1999). Recognize how many artists were inspired by religious faith – as well as by payment from a client.

3 Visit the website of Nicholas Mynheer and look up the luminous Sarum Cycle of paintings. What do they say to you?

4 Look up some of the poets who have been motivated by faith, such as John Milton, George Herbert, T. S. Eliot, R. S. Thomas. Read and reflect on a number of their poems. What is it that comes through their poetry – what emotions, struggles, desires?

5 You might try reading Mark's Gospel as a work of literature conveying faith. Mark is the shortest and earliest Gospel and tells the story vividly, combining both passion and artistry.

10

'Coming home'

A need to belong

———•◦•———

'Sometimes I feel like an orphan always searching for a home.'

'Where can you find real community these days?'

'I feel quite wistful now when I go into a church.'

* * *

I remember a young mother saying to me once, 'When I started coming to church I didn't know if I believed in God. Now I come regularly, and I do.' She had discovered something special through being part of a community which was probably made up of confident believers, half-believers, maybe-believers, and only-on-a-Sunday believers. But that community had been shaped by a story that has proved compellingly attractive and powerful to millions of people all over the world for two millennia, and somewhere near the centre of the story has been the necessary formation of human groups, motley families of disparate individuals dedicated to the well-being of others.

Our culture prides itself on being inclusive but the evidence is otherwise. We love being exclusive. We put the highest price tickets on exclusive homes, holidays, cars, restaurants, clothes, etc., all of which are expressly designed to exclude people who are 'not one of us', that is, poorer, less successful, less cool. There are major cities in most countries where you can see the rich, wealthy and powerful living on one side of a main road, and on the other side the poor, unemployed and marginalized. The problem is that no one crosses the road. There's no common bond, no sense of community. Apparently the most visited place in the world is the Dubai Mall, which has 80 million visitors a year. It has 14 miles of shopfronts compared with one and a half miles in London's Oxford Street. It's clearly a success story of sorts but it represents the victory of a business model based on wealthy foreigners, cheap credit, even cheaper labour, and the absence of rights and freedoms. It's a parable of a world becoming ever more unequal and segregated. It demonstrates the apartheid of wealth and it condemns us to chronic individualism and loneliness.

Such shopping malls are the new cathedrals of consumption and they're devoid of any sense of belonging to a community or a higher vision. They serve individual acquisitiveness. By contrast, the purpose of the cathedrals, churches and holy places of the world's great faiths is precisely to foster community around a distinctive, compelling vision. The sense of belonging to a community is one of the great hungers of the age. We want to know where home is, where we are known by name and valued simply as human beings worthy of dignity and respect. One of the few places left in western society where community flourishes and acts as a hub for substantial social engagement, is the local church, synagogue, mosque or other holy place. And it seems that the holiness is an important element. It provides the fuel for commitment.

Places of prayer are traditionally centres of hospitality and sanctuary. The holy places I know best are churches and I love the way they stand, silently available, in every neighbourhood, town and village in the land. They're there for those who want to belong to the life of the current community, as well as for those who want to belong to a deeper, quieter community that stretches across the centuries and even across the divide of death. Journalist Camilla Cavendish went to church after her mother died:

> The first Sunday after she [Camilla's mother] went I felt an overwhelming urge to go and light a candle in church. This surprised me. But it seemed immeasurably powerful

compared with anything else I had done. That flicker of the eternal, of hope, or recognition, was important to me. On the second Sunday I took my children to the local church that we frequent like itinerant travellers, but where we are always greeted without a hint of umbrage. The familiar words and music, the time to reflect, somehow anchored the grief ... I take my children to church from time to time to give them a foundation that might later fill a void. It is undeniable that the yawning gap I feel has been partly assuaged by the church; I cannot quite say by God. My mother couldn't have said that either, although she was heading that way. This was remarkable for a militant rationalist, a woman who powered her way into Oxford University from America in the 1950s, on whose bookshelves Dawkins and Nietzsche are prominent. But they also contain a Bible, with pages marked. She had become a churchgoer. She, like me, had found comfort in the rituals. And perhaps something more.[1]

There seems to be something deep in our individual and corporate memories that predisposes many of us to connect with 'something more' in places like this. We brush against something deep and reassuring, like something we once knew, something like home. It's hard to identify the nature of what's lost and found; in a way it feels better not to try. This is 'a serious house on serious earth' (see the poem at the end of the chapter) and it has its own unutterable language. This is why it's so important that churches are kept open all day, so people can wander in and loiter with no particular intent but be recipients of an unspoken welcome and the awareness of unexpected Presence.

Of course all this can be put down to sentimentality and nostalgia. As ever, these experiences that I'm calling 'something more' are properly ambiguous. They don't prove anything, they merely offer an invitation. It's not my purpose to bludgeon anyone with my interpretation of reality; I simply want to suggest that the exploration of these experiences is worthwhile and exciting. And I suspect that if our culture were less hostile to spiritual interpretations many more people would admit to the persuasive welcome of these special places. I was once approached by a middle-aged visitor after an early morning communion service at Canterbury Cathedral. He said, 'I haven't been to that service for thirty years.' Unsure how to reply, I came out with, 'Welcome home.' Tears came to his eyes. 'That's exactly it,' he said, and left.

I have to admit to some diffidence about the next bit. It's all very well finding our way into an empty church in the week and finding company in the presence of generations gone before, but it's a whole different challenge to enter that same building on Sunday when lots of people are milling around and a complex communal activity is about to start. Nevertheless, this is the living community that can offer a true sense of belonging, the missing keystone of contemporary life. My diffidence is that such communities can easily disappoint us and leave hopeful enquirers disillusioned. We all have feet of clay. Churches are made up of people with the same foibles, irritations, failures and obsessions as everyone else. Ideally they don't say 'that's just the way I am.' Ideally they try to be open to be changed. But it doesn't always work.

I was at church yesterday and sitting behind four young men, intrigued as to where they'd come from, and unable to see the service any way other than through their eyes. What do visitors make of the strange rituals of the average church service? It turned out that they were from a nearby army camp – one was a chaplain, one a Roman Catholic, and two were rather more tangentially related to what was going on. Fortunately they were befriended by the regular congregation over coffee, but my question stayed with me: what would they have made of what we were doing, and of what this community was like? Could they have felt they might belong to a place like this?

There are failures, but in general churches are communities of good people with high ideals, serving the wider community with unaffected generosity and commitment. They're places of sincerity, laughter and mutual care. They don't blow their own trumpet but recognize the privilege and responsibility of having a faith and an opportunity to contribute to the common good. These communities are rooted in a compelling story from the living past, are fully committed to the demanding needs of the present, and are drawn by the vision of a new world in the future – nicknamed the Kingdom of God.

All churches are imperfect because they're made up of imperfect people, but people on a journey, a long journey. Ruth Graham, wife of evangelist Billy, was once caught for hours in a huge traffic jam on a California turnpike. The sign at the end of the traffic jam said, 'Construction ended. Thank you for your patience.' She had that inscribed on her gravestone.

But whatever the eccentricities of the gathered communities of believers (and half-believers, etc.; see above) the experience of worship can still have a mysterious power. People can be moved at an unexpected level by the rhythms of well-ordered, or even well-intentioned, worship. Take this journalist's experience:

> A week ago I attended Evensong at Jesus College, Cambridge, where the Small Boy is a chorister. I hadn't been to church in a while and it took me a few seconds waiting for the faith muscle-memory to kick in. The choir sang. They say the devil has all the best tunes. Well, they're wrong; Jesus has Hubert Parry and Johann Sebastian Bach. We knelt. We stood, then knelt again. We sang 'Immortal, invisible, God only wise'. We turned to face the altar. 'We believe in one God, the Father Almighty, maker of heaven and earth.' I'm not sure what I believe, but I do know every word of the creed, and when I say them I feel I am joining myself to generations who spoke those words centuries before I was born, and that custom is deeply consoling ... Religion is strange, infinitely mysterious and easy to mock, but all I can say is that its rituals feel full, not hollow, as so much of modern life does.[2]

Certainly, this was an elite act of worship in a rarefied context, but it illustrates how worship can connect us, anchor us, and offer an experience of sufficiency and fulfilment. Whether the community we join is one of the past in an empty church on a weekday visit, or of the present on a Sunday morning in worship, these are places of belonging where we might just find ourselves in contact with that mysterious 'something more'.

Key question

What have we got to lose by going to church with an open mind and seeing how the whole experience feels?

Tips for church leaders

These are some down-to-earth tips offered to church leaders by Linda Woodhead, Professor of Sociology of Religion at Lancaster University, to enhance people's experience of going to church:[3]

- Most services are too long and too wordy. People want space to find God. Try not to fill it up with distractions.
- There are people who want to hover round the edges of religion: to look at the graves; sit in an empty church; go to the carol service; run a club. Make sure there are ways people can engage at all levels.
- Leaders: be open about your doubts and fears.
- If a lay person can do it better, let her/him.
- If you are a preacher or teacher, express yourself clearly, and make your point in five minutes.
- Liturgy works when it's not too relaxed and not too formal. Aim for relaxed formality.
- Don't claim overfamiliarity with God.
- Remember that people love to learn new skills.
- A lot of people aren't looking for community. They're looking for a break from it.

- Churches work when they offer wholeness and holiness.
- Churches grow when they offer people life-giving connection with the sacred.
- Church buildings have things people treasure: history, beauty, continuity. Find ways to let people reconnect with them.
- Churches grow when they give people voice and choice.
- Churches should be much more upfront about what they offer. People need to know what they're getting.

Poem: Church Going

Once I am sure there's nothing going on
I step inside, letting the door thud shut.
Another church: matting, seats, and stone,
For Sunday, brownish now; some brass and stuff
Up at the holy end; the small neat organ;
And a tense, musty, unignorable silence,
Brewed God knows how long. Hatless, I take off
My cycle clips in awkward reverence.

Move forward, run my hand around the font.
From where I stand, the roof looks almost new –
Cleaned, or restored? Someone would know: I don't.
Mounting the lectern, I peruse a few
Hectoring large-scale verses, and pronounce
'Here endeth' more loudly than I'd meant.
The echoes snigger briefly. Back at the door
I sign the book, donate an Irish sixpence,
Reflect the place was not worth stopping for.

Yet stop I did: in fact I often do,
And always end much at a loss like this,
Wondering what to look for; wondering, too,
When churches will fall completely out of use
What we shall turn them into, if we shall keep
A few cathedrals chronically on show,
Their parchment, plate and pyx in locked cases,

And let the rest rent-free to rain and sheep.
Shall we avoid them as unlucky places?

. . .

A serious house in serious earth it is,
In whose blent air all our compulsions meet,
Are recognised, and robed as destinies.
And that much never can be obsolete,
Since someone will forever be surprising
A hunger in himself to be more serious,
And gravitate with it to this ground,
Which, he once heard, was proper to grow wise in,
If only that so many dead lie around.

Philip Larkin[4]

Taking it further

If you want to think a little further about this kind of experience, here are some things you might like to do:

1 Sneak into a church midweek. Explore it, smell it and feel it. Sit and listen to the silence. Stay there longer than you thought you would. What feelings does it arouse?
2 Perhaps try a service on Sunday and sit near a pillar. Let the service flow over you, without judgement. Afterwards, think what was positive about the experience. Go again . . .
3 Some possible books to read:

- Timothy Radcliffe, *Why Go To Church?* (London: Continuum, 2009)
- Francis Spufford, *Unapologetic* (London: Faber and Faber, 2012)
- John Pritchard, *Going to Church: A User's Guide* (London: SPCK, 2009)

4 Read 1 Corinthians 12.12—13.13. Paul helps this early church in Corinth to value every member, and in particular to value the supreme gift of love when living together in community.

11

'Why is there something rather than nothing?'

A need for answers

———•◆•———

'We're bound to have a scientific world-view these days, so what place is there for religion?'

'I just can't be satisfied that my child is merely an accidental collection of DNA and neural pathways.'

'Big questions need big answers.'

* * *

I've always felt that our highest allegiance should be to the truth, wherever that leads us. I happen to believe that if you pursue the truth avidly and long enough you bump into a reality some of us call God, but that isn't the point. The point is that the pursuit of intellectually satisfying answers to life's big questions is very important to many of us. And the biggest questions are where science, philosophy and theology interact. I'm aware that the relationship of science and religion isn't an itch that everyone wants to scratch, but equally I know that for some people this is where the hardest questions about life, the universe and everything are to be found. Unless some progress can be made here, all bets are off.

It's often assumed that science has pushed religion out of the front stalls and relegated it to a little chair in the corridor. The two were in conflict and science won. This is sadly the unexamined assumption many people make today. A rather more nuanced approach sees science and religion as complementary, with science taking things apart to see how they work and religion putting things together to see what they mean. Take a boiling kettle. *How* is it boiling? Because electricity is causing a heat exchange which is raising the temperature of the water and that in turn is causing an observable change in its state. But *why* is it boiling? Because I want a cup of coffee. The latter is the question of meaning, and these 'why' questions can't just be reduced to 'how' questions. The two do, however, overlap, and it's important not to over-simplify these complex issues. As Einstein said, 'Everything should be made as simple as possible, but not simpler.'[1]

So let's take the discussion further and explore the overlap of scientific explanations and religious thought in terms of dialogue and integration. Thoughtful people will then ask themselves a number of questions. For example, the perennial 'why is there something rather than nothing?' The known laws of physics were operating nanoseconds after the Big Bang, but the unimaginable explosion of the universe from its original singularity requires some explanation. Scientists have suggested fluctuations in the quantum vacuum, but this only pushes the question further back – why is there a quantum vacuum? A multiverse theory has gained much popular leverage; if you have an infinity of universes, one of them is bound to produce the carbon-based life we now know, on the familiar, far-fetched analogy of monkeys typing endlessly on keyboards being bound eventually to produce the works of Shakespeare. Alternatively there could have been not so much a Big Bang as a 'Big Bounce', with our universe being a rebound from a defunct previous universe. But the irritating question is never vanquished – why the singularity, why the quantum vacuum, why the previous universe?

The philosophical principle of Ockham's razor seems applicable: if there are competing explanations for something, the simpler one should be preferred. God is the simpler explanation, but not God as Divine Interferer, turning the original switch; rather God the background rationality to everything, the ground of the cosmological processes. Physicist John Polking-horne sees it like this:

> The world that science describes seems to me, with its order, intelligibility, potentiality and tightly knit character, to be one that is consonant with the idea that it is the expression of the will of a Creator, subtle, patient, and content to achieve his purposes by the slow unfolding of process inherent in those laws of nature which, in their regularity, are but the pale reflections of his abiding faithfulness.[2]

God is in this view the unchanging rational ground in which the logically ordered nature of the universe is rooted. Or, as the philosopher Kierkegaard put it, 'God does not exist; he is eternal.'

This begs another question: has religious language any meaning in the discussion of these issues, or is it just fine-sounding obfuscation? Here it looks as if we have a choice. If we are asking how existence can come out of non-existence, we might operate entirely with a materialist world-view *or* we might admit we are in the realm of the metaphysical, i.e. the large-scale philosophical groundwork of existence. I would contend that science can't do away with metaphysics or philosophy; assumptions about the nature of being are inevitable, and are best examined in the open rather than ignored because they're uncomfortable. So, in the context of metaphysics, belief in eternal, necessary and self-sustaining Mind is a reasonable approach to the most profound questions, including the search for a Grand Unifying Theory that holds together both cosmological and quantum thinking.

I said it looks as if we have a choice between materialist and metaphysical approaches, but they don't actually need to be in competition; they just don't need to rubbish each other. Ted Harrison notes how, when we get to the further reaches of cosmology, the language scientists use moves into image and metaphor, almost parable. 'Cosmologists talk of the big bang, or bangs, as being like bubbles in a Swiss cheese, or like a bounce, or like two multi-dimensional membranes touching.' Jesus talked about the Kingdom of God being like a mustard seed, or a fine pearl, or yeast, or treasure hidden in a field, or a net thrown into the sea. Analogy is common ground, as well as the language of elegance, symmetry, beauty and wonder.

Indeed, Ted Harrison points out, cosmologists are on the verge of astonishing discoveries, 'producing not only the biggest picture yet, "but the biggest picture possible".' And that, he reminds us, is rather like St Anselm's eleventh-century definition of God: 'That than which nothing greater can be conceived.'[3]

There is plenty of evidence, therefore, that a conflict theory between science and religion is unnecessary. The one thing to avoid is writing off the wisdom of the other, as Christian creationists do so lamentably, especially in the United States. Equally, scientists need to resist the temptations of omniscience. The author Howard Jacobson, an agnostic, wrote, 'Nothing returns one quicker to God than the sight of a scientist with no imagination, no vocabulary, no sympathy, no comprehension of metaphor, and no wit, looking soulless and forlorn amid the wonders of nature.'[4]

There are huge questions here and it isn't my purpose to try and answer them, only to point out their potential for further exploration. Modern cosmology has served to put our finitude in perspective as tiny spectators in the cosmic circus, but at the same time has placed us more firmly in the ring where the performers operate. We know that if the earth was formed at midnight the day before yesterday, on the evolutionary clock we would only be emerging on the last stroke of midnight today. But at the same time the 'anthropic principle' points to a series of cosmological coincidences that have allowed intelligent life to emerge, the statistical *un*likelihood of which is such that 'it almost seems as if the universe must in some sense have known we were coming'.[5] It seems as if there is some sort of purpose in operation and we are meant to be here. We have prime seats.

Moreover a reductionist, materialist view of our place in the universe leaves many human capacities without adequate explanation – above all, self-awareness and our capacity for love, creativity, wonder, evil, moral behaviour and transcendence. We can do to creation what it can't do to us – we can think about it. In us, the universe becomes conscious of itself. Evolutionary biology has a stab at explaining these phenomena but to many people such explanations are helpful but not sufficient. Our experience of ourselves, and the range and depth of our emotions, need a further language of purpose and meaning to do justice to their complexity.

It's enough to make you think ... Or at least I hope it is. These are big issues and they need big answers.

At the other end of the size spectrum from cosmology is the tiny world of quantum theory. Quantum mechanics examines the world at the subatomic level and it has been said that if we aren't shocked by quantum thinking we haven't understood it.[6] The world of Newtonian physics was predictable and described the real world as we perceive it. Quantum theory discloses a world that is random and unpredictable and where most of what we thought of as solid is in fact empty space. It's a world where light is both a wave and a particle depending on how we view it. It's a world where every particle in the universe knows about every other, where the behaviour of a particle is uncertain until it is observed and thereby forced into one of many possibilities, a world which is open to chance as well as necessity.

For some people quantum theory is another nail in God's coffin. If the world is random, blind and uncaring, then how can God be a loving, creative presence at its heart? How can God be OK with unpredictability and uncertainty and still be Lord of the universe? On the other hand, you could say that it was the steel doors of Newtonian physics that drove God off the map because you could give an account of reality without leaving any room for divine presence and activity, whereas a quantum world is much more open-ended and God can be a player in it as the ultimate determiner behind apparent indeterminacy. It opens the door to human beings as free agents who know they are loved and whose actions matter, where prayer becomes meaningful as a contributory factor to the ways things turn out, and where even miracle cannot be ruled out of order because the unexpected is part of the way the world is. The open texture of the quantum universe is a much more congenial space for a dialogue between science and religion. Paul Dirac, the British physicist noted for his pioneering work in quantum physics, wrote that 'God used beautiful mathematics in creating the world'.[7]

Put in the simplest way possible, the questions that deserve continuing exploration are probably these:

1 Why is there something rather than nothing?
2 Where do the scientific laws underlying the universe come from?
3 Why is the universe intelligible?
4 Why is the universe so finely balanced to bring forth life?
5 Why do people find the universe so awe-inspiring?

None of the questions require a theistic answer. As ever, there's no compulsion. Nor would it serve God well if there were knock-down proofs of God's being, because that would remove our most fundamental freedom not to believe. But the questions that have teased serious thinkers for centuries might at least give us pause. How we handle them will be the consequence of a number of factors, ranging from our intellectual interest to our world-view.

This is not the place for a proper exploration of these complex issues, even if I were competent to offer it, which I clearly am not. What matters here is that there are fascinating questions to be explored for those who need to add intellectual grist to the spiritual mill, and that contemporary debates between science and religion are alive and well, and for some, open up possibilities of belief that they didn't think were available.

Just don't expect to understand it all . . .

Key question

Is a materialist account of the universe sufficient by itself?

Story

A vicar went to visit a young couple who wanted to be married. They lived in a caravan where the bride-to-be had been born and lived all her life. Communication was stilted, but the bride was clear that marriage in church was the right thing and that God was somehow involved. The groom was quiet but admitted that he wasn't sure about God. As the vicar left he put his hand in his pocket and found a hazelnut he had picked up in his garden. He handed it to the groom and said, 'Here's something to think about – who put the life into this nut?'

When the vicar returned a week later the young man greeted him with the words, 'I haven't been able to sleep since you last came with that nut question. I can't answer it.' It was the start of a spiritual journey that led to baptism, confirmation and an ongoing faith.[8]

To think about

The older I get, the more I find I am returning to those deep questions and asking 'Why?' I don't think it's enough to shrug this question aside. We do want to know why the world is as it is. Why did it come to exist 13.7 billion years ago in a Big Bang? Why are the laws of electromagnetism and gravitation as they are? Why those laws? What are we doing here? And in particular, how come we are able to understand the world? Why is it that we're equipped with intellects that can unpick all this wonderful cosmic order and make sense of it? It's truly astonishing.

Paul Davies, cosmologist[9]

The incomprehensible thing about the universe is that it is comprehensible.   Albert Einstein, mathematician[10]

Why does the universe go to all the bother of existing?

Stephen Hawking, cosmologist[11]

Taking it further

This is deep stuff and not for the faint-hearted, but here are some things you might do:

1 There are many accessible ways in to the subject of science and religion. For example:

- Gillian K. Straine, *Introducing Science and Religion* (London: SPCK, 2014)
- John C. Lennox, *God's Undertaker* (Oxford: Lion, 2007)
- R. J. Berry (ed.), *The Lion Handbook of Science and Christianity* (Oxford: Lion, 2012)
- Any books on the subject by John Polkinghorne, Francis Collins, Alister McGrath

2 Get in touch with the vicar of any large local church and ask if they have a science teacher in their congregation. Ask to meet and talk.

3 Read Genesis 1.1—2.3, not for the science but for the poetry, the parable and the underlying message.

12

'Darkness at noon'

The sudden collapse of our world

'All of a sudden I was living a nightmare.'

'Nothing could have prepared me for this.'

'I don't know how we coped.'

* * *

Some of the most poignant services I ever take part in are those that commemorate the victims of road traffic accidents. Emotions are tender as we pick our way carefully through fragile memories. I talk to the relatives afterwards and hear of the normal morning routines that ended with the usual carefree goodbye as the loved one swept out of the house for good, the door shutting on an entire life of shared experiences, joys and dreams. The jagged tragedy had ripped through the familiar fabric of life they had thought so secure and reliable.

What now? How do you cope when your world suddenly collapses?

There's sometimes a moment when a parent, a partner, a lover, a friend realizes that everything is about to change catastrophically. The sight of two police officers coming up the path; the calamitous noise of something crashing to the ground; the news announcement that clutches at the throat because you know instinctively it involves you. With a sickening lurch you know that you're about to enter a nightmare. Already you find you're looking back nostalgically at the sanity and security of your world as it was just a minute ago.

Sometimes the life-changing experience isn't sudden, but rather your recognition of the seriousness of the dread event grows steadily as the nightmare darkens. Many relatives of victims of 9/11 or the London bombings in July 2007 endured the agonizing wait for news of a loved one as the clock crawled its way through the day and no reassuring phone call came. When a plane goes missing somewhere in the world, television pictures remorselessly expose the growing panic of relatives waiting at the airport.

And there are personal crises too, which assume horrific proportions in the recesses of the night when fear runs amok through our defenceless minds. Is it cancer? What will that mean? Could they have got it wrong? How long have I got? How will I measure up? Please let it all be a dream ...

I can remember the precise place I was standing when I received serious news about one of our daughters, and on another occasion, about the daughter of close friends. Those moments that changed everything are etched on my memory. I remember another moment when I felt really ill with chest pains, palpitations, sickness and an intense headache, and I feared that, even at my then young age, I might be about to have a heart attack. I looked through the window at two men talking in the sunny courtyard outside and wondered why they weren't bothered about this impending tragedy. These are life-shredding experiences, and they're carved on my mind as moments when a nightmare walked right in through my front door and possessed the whole house.

It's easy to be melodramatic, but most of us have had these experiences of panic and the question is posed in stark relief: What resources have I got to handle this? We might find ourselves reaching out for something, anything, that offers even a faltering glimmer of hope. It's why we look up every possible treatment on the internet, or become an avid consumer of homeopathic remedies, or grasp at any story of recovery that friends tell us. It's why a bereaved person might turn to spiritualism in a desperate attempt to contact his or her loved one. It's why some people turn towards faith.

There's a somewhat over-simplified refrain that goes like this: 'Fear knocked at the door. Faith answered. There was nobody there.' There's reliable experience behind that little refrain; down the years countless people have found that faith is one of the most effective ways to counter fear. But it can't be made into a sugary promise. The black crows of doubt will always circle overhead and the struggle to carry on when tragedy has completely winded a person will inevitably continue for a long time. Nevertheless, the concrete surface of our secular world-view is often broken open by fear, and new thoughts and ideas can emerge.

The fundamental spiritual question is about the presence or possibility of some reliable, stable point around which I can regroup. Is there a place beyond fear? Do I have any firm reference points to hold me, or for me to hold on to? The alternative is to be tossed around on the high seas of random crises and cling to the resulting wreckage, nobly resisting fate. Such stoicism is not to be despised. If faith is an impossible move for someone to explore, then heroic resilience is better than whimpering in a corner.

And yet, this is surely a time when faith might at least be allowed a voice. The Christian contribution is expressed by Rowan Williams in this way:

> At the heart of the desperate suffering there is in the world, suffering we can do nothing to resolve or remove for good, there is an indestructible energy making for love. If we have grasped what Jesus is about, we can trust that this is what lies at the foundation of everything.[1]

This is not Christianity claiming to make intellectual or even emotional and spiritual sense of the nightmare, but it is to claim that the universe has a redemptive heart, 'an indestructible energy making for love', and that this cosmic kindness is to be trusted.

At the heart of tragedy may be an opening to this 'something more' of a redemptive energy which is inexhaustible and which will never stop trying to fashion hope from the raw material of fear, panic and grief. Faith, therefore, is not an evasion of the darkness but a deeper entry into it, in order to be the yeast that works unseen with the reluctant dough and produces something of more lasting value. Tragedy is still tragedy, but the 'indestructible energy' of Love may yet incubate a gritty hope or a tender beauty in the one who suffers. We may begin to believe we'll come through.

Key question

Is there a place beyond fear? Do you have any firm reference points to hold you, or for you to hold on to, in times of crisis?

Poem: Learning to breathe under water

I built my house by the sea.
Not on the sands, mind you,
not on the shifting sand.
And I built it of rock.
A strong house
by a strong sea.
And we got well acquainted, the sea and I.
Good neighbours,
Not that we spoke much.
We met in silences,
respectful, keeping our distance
but looking our thoughts across the fence of sand.
Always the fence of sand our barrier,
Always the sand between.
And then one day
(and I still don't know how it happened)

The sea came.

Without warning.

Without welcome even.

Not sudden and swift, but a shifting across the sand like wine,

less like the flow of water than the flow of blood.

Slow, but like an open wound.

And I thought of flight, and I thought of drowning, and I thought of
death.

But while I thought, the sea crept higher till it reached my door.

And I knew then that there was neither flight nor death nor drowning.

That when the sea comes calling you stop being good neighbours,

Well acquainted, friendly from a distance neighbours.

And you give your house for a coral castle

And you learn to breathe under water.   Carole Bialock[2]

To think about

God is to be trusted as we would trust a loving parent,
whose commitment to us is inexhaustible, whose pur-
poses for us are unfailingly generous; someone whose life
is the source of our life, and who guarantees there is always
a home for us.   Rowan Williams[3]

Taking it further

If this experience rings any bells, then the following might be
worth considering:

1 The practice of mindfulness is now well established as an
   effective way of countering panic, anxiety, depression and
   other forms of distress. Based on Buddhist (and Christian)
   meditation practice, mindfulness enables the person using
   it to attend to the present moment and to be aware of her
   or his distress but not consumed by it. Mindfulness is widely
   used in schools, industry, the NHS, even the Houses of

Parliament. There's ample information on the internet. One well-used book is *Mindfulness: A Practical Guide to Finding Peace in a Frantic World* by Mark Williams and Danny Penman (London: Piatkus, 2011), but there are many others, including *Mindfulness and Christian Spirituality* by Tim Stead (London: SPCK, 2016). Apart from the emotional benefit, the practice of mindfulness might open up an interest in its spiritual background and give access to the larger world of the religious traditions that have sustained the majority of the world's population for centuries.

2 It can help to go to a place where there's a track record of security and solidity, such as a church, to which generations of people have taken their fears and found prayer to be valid. I once encountered a man ruminating in the cloisters of Canterbury Cathedral and he said he came back occasionally because some years ago 'this place saved my life'. I didn't press him, but he said he'd reached the end of the road and coming here had stopped him doing anything drastic. Churches hold in a quiet, reassuring embrace everything that's brought to them. They don't panic; they've seen it all before. They accept our deepest needs without question and place them in a richer, deeper story where they are held safely.

3 The metaphor of God as a rock is a favourite image in the Bible, offered when either Israel or the individual believer is in trouble, under attack or in despair. The image is a particular favourite in the Psalms and can be found throughout the collection, for example 'The LORD is my rock, my fortress, and my deliverer, my God, my rock in whom I take refuge' (Ps. 18.2); 'He drew me up from the desolate pit, out of the miry bog, and set my feet upon a rock, making my steps secure' (Ps. 40.2). There are many other such references throughout the Psalms and other books of the Bible. It might help to rest with that image, to internalize it, and to see if it makes sense to believe that at rock bottom there is Rock.

13

'Hatching, matching, dispatching'

Unexpected discoveries

'It felt like I'd opened a door I never knew – or I'd forgotten – was there.'

'From being confidently self-sufficient, I found I needed help from somewhere.'

'There was suddenly so much I wanted to know.'

* * *

As we travel through our late twenties and thirties, life usually settles into something of a rhythm. Most of us have acquired some shape to our lives in terms of career, friendships, partner, lifestyle, etc., and without realizing it a thin veneer of concrete has probably settled over our way of life, our habits, beliefs and values. It then needs some fairly major event to disrupt those patterns and to break up the concrete so that something new can come through. Often this is the arrival of a child, but it could be a final decision to get married or, sadly, it could be an accident or a tragic death.

Our previous experiences will have shaped our core view of the world, and this working model then acts like an invisible lens through which we assess the world we see before us and in which we operate day to day. The lens is the more powerful because we aren't aware of it. This world-view will affect everything from how we react to political events to what we do on a Saturday night, and with whom. It gives us security because within the 'world of the world-view' we know our way around.

We know what we think is of value, how we want to behave, and what we want to spend our money on. It's a tough nut to crack.

But then along comes a child, and it's astonishing. One sperm out of three hundred million has reached and invaded an ovum some eighty-five thousand times its own size, and the result is this miraculous, fully functioning, red, scrawny, adorable bundle you might hold in one open hand. There were a million other lives that could have been born but this is the one that made it. And you would give your life for it. The depth of feeling this little thing generates takes your breath away. Normal, tough young men become doting uncles, as Caitlin Moran described in an article:

> They were amazing babysitters: there's something moving about very young men looking after tiny girls – carrying tiny, pink lunchboxes to nursery with a small, hysterically laughing ballerina on their shoulders. They insisted on calling my daughters 'Bernard' and 'Dave': 'If anyone ever makes you cry, Dave, we will come round and end them,' they would tell the tiny, round-faced, cross-eyed child on their knee.[1]

The arrival of children is a world-changing event, and many parents are taken aback by the profundity of the experience. They then find they need to mark it in some way, to honour the gift, to pledge absolute love, care and protection to this precious little responsibility, and to do so in the most significant context and setting they can find. Which is where baptism (popularly called 'christening') comes surprisingly into view. The beliefs of the parents and godparents may be fairly rudimentary – it would be hard for most parents to account adequately for the need and appropriateness of this ceremony – but they feel there's a spiritual context here that seems oddly right for such a life-changing experience as having a child. The service might be noisy and chaotic (the noisiest child I ever baptized was my own daughter) but the ritual is strangely important. The concrete is broken open; just possibly a spiritual journey might begin.

In a sense marriage is less of an interruption than having a child. Nevertheless, it's a very significant step that digs down beneath the topsoil of our lives and unearths our fundamental needs and aspirations. It too can be a shock, even if, as is usually the case, the couple have been together for a considerable time. Marriage is like using chopsticks, twirling a baton or doing handsprings – it looks easy until you try. It marks the transition from experiment to commitment and it asks us to hedge our bets no longer. During a correspondence on pre-nuptial contracts, a man wrote to the letters page of *The Times* saying, 'Sir, My wife Miriam and myself made a pre-nuptial contract in which we decided that if she ever left me she would take me with her. This has been highly successful. We celebrated our 62nd wedding anniversary last December.' This is the kind of commitment that marriage alarmingly assumes, and because it's so demanding many people want to take it to the highest court of significance they can. They go to church.

Of course this is no guarantee of success, but at least it indicates, hopefully, a high degree of seriousness. And, again, a crack appears in the concrete and some couples find their spiritual antennae are activated. At our church last week a couple came with their small daughter from over thirty miles away, because this is where they got married and the connection they formed at that period of their lives is one they value enough to get up at half past six on a Sunday morning to give themselves time to drive that far. A spiritual journey is under way. Clergy aren't naïve enough not to realize that some people come to church for a wedding because it's pretty, traditional, atmospheric, nice for photographs, etc., but the door has been opened a crack and it's up to the church to offer its warmest hospitality and to see what happens as a result of the whole experience. A Church of England Weddings Project a few years ago found a very high level of 'consumer satisfaction' from those who had got married in church. It doesn't matter if they don't immediately become regular churchgoers; it's the offering of a significant spiritual context to one of life's major transitions that matters, and then it's up to what believers describe as the Holy Spirit.

Death is, obviously, the great interrupter of our lives. The French philosopher Albert Camus described it as 'the dark wind blowing from my future'.[2] It has a 100 per cent success rate and the prospect catches all of us off guard at some point. Death always leaves someone in tears, married or single, and however many funerals I take my heart always goes out to the people whose lives have been ripped open by this loss – this was holy ground. But there can be a strange fruit from this tragic experience. I've known many people who have found their way into a community of faith after bereavement, first perhaps for consolation, but then from conviction as they found the spiritual and social realities they encountered to be genuinely liberating. Some people have a more dramatic experience. I knew a man who was sitting in the crematorium after the funeral of his wife, and he felt a very definite wind, warm and knowing, spring up from nowhere and surround him. It was somehow deeply reassuring but he didn't act on it for two months. He wanted to allow the reassurance to wither if it was an illusion. But when the experience remained true he took it to a context that he felt could hold it. He went to church and has remained there ever since.

Serious illness is another 'before and after' experience that can have a profound influence on our lives. Recovery can lead to a significant reappraisal of assumptions and priorities. The philosopher Victor Frankl was once declared clinically dead but then recovered and afterwards wrote:

> Suddenly everything gets precious, gets piercingly important. You get stabbed by things – by flowers and babies and by beautiful things; just the very act of living, of walking and breathing, of eating, having friends and chatting. Suddenly there are miracles everywhere.[3]

Most of us can imagine the truth of those observations. 'Everything gets precious . . . there are miracles everywhere.' It's a hard way to an awakening, but what Frankl discovered was what is actually available all the time – a world of miracles. I was once preparing to undertake a 100-mile pilgrimage along the Thames, but in trying to get fitter than my usually sedentary job allowed I found I was experiencing alarming chest pains. The upshot was an angiogram that revealed 75–95 per cent blockage in a vital artery and the implanting of an immediate stent. Six days later I went on the pilgrimage and was moved by the joy of walking, the freshness of the colours, the swish of the grasses, the sunniness of the sun and the sheer 'is-ness' of things. I try now not to take all that for granted.

There are other interruptions of life that crack open the concrete and allow a tender spiritual plant to grow through. Unemployment, divorce, children leaving home, even a house move, all these can have a similar effect, though nothing is guaranteed; there need be no spiritual response, the concrete may be too well set. But if something is glimpsed through this unfamiliar, life-changing experience it might be worth following it up. The concrete will harden again fairly quickly, but what if what was glimpsed at that moment was in fact worth every penny we have?

Key question

Has our experience of a birth, marriage, death, or any other transition, brought us up against any bigger questions about life, its source and meaning?

Story

In his teenage years, TV adventurer Bear Grylls found himself profoundly affected by a death:

It was around 16 I found my Christian faith. I wasn't brought up in the church but I had a natural faith when I was a little kid; I always believed in something. Then when I went to school I thought, if there is a God surely he doesn't speak Latin and stand in a pulpit? But when I was 16 my godfather, who was like a second parent to me, died. I was really upset and I said a very simple prayer up a tree – if you're still there, will you just be beside me. And that was the start of something that grew and grew and it's become the backbone of my life. I'm more convinced than ever, no matter how crazy it sounds, that there is a God and he is love. It's a very personal relationship; I still don't go to church very much. But to this day I start every day on my knees praying by my bed, and that's my grounding for the day. Believing in God definitely makes me less scared in life in general. People say I'm not scared of anything. Well, I am, I'm scared of lots of things. After my sky-diving accident in the military [a fall doctors feared would paralyse him for life] I still have to parachute quite a lot and I find that hard. But having a faith reduces my fear hugely because I'm not alone, I'm fighting these battles with the creator and that's amazing. My faith definitely plays a part in my love of the outdoors – I see miracles everywhere I look, in mountains and in the jungle. And I think I have less of a fear of death as well because I see it as going home.　　　　Bear Grylls[4]

To think about

Be aware of the fact that what you are saying now, doing now, hearing, enduring or receiving now may be the last event or experience of your present life. In which case it must be a crowning, not a defeat; a summit, not a trough. All life is, at every moment, an ultimate act.

Metropolitan Anthony Bloom[5]

Taking it further

If any of this echoes with your experience, it might be worthwhile trying some of the following:

1 Find a church that has a beginners' group of some kind where you can ask questions and discuss basic issues. Courses to look out for could be Pilgrim, Alpha, Christianity Explored. Don't let the group stifle your questions!

2 Ask any Christian you know to come out for a drink or a meal, and ask her direct questions about how she got started in her faith and why she goes to church and what she believes about God. Make your questions bold ones.

3 Try reading a book on core Christian faith, such as:

- Rowan Williams, *Tokens of Trust* (London: Canterbury Press, 2007)
- Tom Wright, *Simply Good News* (London: SPCK, 2015)
- John Pritchard, *Beginning Again* (London: SPCK, 2000)
- Timothy Radcliffe, *What is the Point of Being a Christian?* (London: Continuum, 2005).

14

'He hath a daily beauty'
The influence of special people

———◆·◆·◆———

'I owe her more than she'll ever know.'

'I guess I always wanted to be a bit like him.'

'What's she on?'

* * *

I wonder if you know people who make you want to be a better person? I know a number of them; they seem to show up my behaviour and motives like a table of slightly shoddy goods at a jumble sale. Not that these people intend to do any such thing. On the contrary, they seem to believe in me and see good in me I've never noticed. But I still feel, like Iago said of Cassio, 'He hath a daily beauty in his life that makes me ugly.'[1] And it leaves me wanting to be better.

Our normal strategy in facing the world is to have a variety of masks for different audiences. This enables us to function with reasonable success in most settings, though occasionally you feel someone has seen through the mask and is looking at you with particular curiosity. There are masks for work colleagues, for the boss, for smart occasions and for parties, masks for church if we go there, even a light mask for family, though that often slips. Living without a mask is a dangerous experiment, not to be recommended.

The actor Robin Williams was particularly hard to understand because he had so many masks. When he died it was said of him:

In person, interviewers found a polite, softly spoken man, who – when he wasn't breaking into impersonations – came across as rather sad. Friends described him as either somewhat reserved or always 'on', which made him hard to get to know. Once he recalled reading his favourite book, C. S. Lewis's *The Lion, the Witch and the Wardrobe*, to his daughter, Zelda. Usually, when reading aloud to his children, he performed all the voices, but this time 'she said: "Don't do any voices. Just read it as yourself." So I did, I just read it straight, and she said: "That's better."'[2]

Special people make it easier for us to come out from behind the masks we adopt and appear as ourselves, with all our vulner-abilities, but also our gifts and goodness. Above all, we come out as the unique human being we are. Zelda helped her father to do that. Those in our own hall of fame help us to do that too.

We can only be true to our own experience, and mine has been that many of those special people in my own life have been people of faith. In a sense that's obvious because my life as a 'professional believer' has ensured I meet a lot of other believers. But my public roles have also ensured that I've met very large numbers of other people outside faith circles, and I've been delighted to meet good, honest, likeable and talented people everywhere. But the ones who have made the most impression on me have often been people who quietly hum with an earthy holiness. I think of some of them now, enjoying life to the full, responding to anything beautiful with delight, sitting lightly to their dignity, laughing often. They're full of life but their energy seems to emanate from an inner stillness, as if their deepest focus is elsewhere. They're relaxed with them-selves and with others; children are often instinctively at home with them. They don't share the preoccupation with ourselves that marks our culture; they're interested in you, indeed in everything. They get straight to the point, and they want us to get there too. They seem somehow to be amphibious – at home in the thick of everyday life, and at the same time at home in the world of 'angels and archangels and all the company of heaven'. At its simplest, these people are just good to be with. You smile when you see them.

Do you know anyone like that? It's a privilege to do so, though occasionally unnerving – as I have already said – when they seem to be able to see through you. This is partly, I think, because sometimes we can actually see through *them*, and what lies beyond is light from a far country. When you look at figures in a stained-glass window you see the vibrant colours of the person depicted there, but you're also seeing the effect of pure light on coloured glass, pouring through from the source of all light, the sun. Our special people are often like that, I would maintain, shown in all their beautiful colours because, without realizing it, they somehow let the light of truth and eternity shine through them.

I've found that if I ask anyone how they started on their spiritual journey, there has nearly always been a significant figure who so fully embodied the journey (let's say, the Christian faith) that they made it possible and attractive to believe. It might have been a youth worker, a curate, a family friend, or, later in life, a spouse, a work colleague, even someone met on a train. These are people who make it easier to believe in God. I know someone who worked for a while in Africa with a doctor who spoke with equal conviction both of his faith and of the roughage children needed in their diet, and whose authenticity in both subjects spoke volumes to his younger colleague.

I think of an elderly woman of distinguished background whose particular gift was that of encouragement – I went to see her often. I think of a man of wide interests and lightly worn learning who always spoke the truth with humour and love. I think of a woman whose deep kindness disguised a determined core of faith and purpose that always looked to the well-being of her community. I think of a man of integrity and intelligence to whom I would trust my life if I needed help. There are many more in my hall of fame. Some are still with us; some are long gone in earthly terms, but if they have indeed departed this life they're rather like the embers of a fire, continuing to give off heat and light to illuminate my journey, and doubtless the journeys of others.

Perhaps we can be challenged by the memory of these people and the question of whether we give out any heat and light, such that someone else might say they have been touched by 'something more'.

Sometimes these special people are unusual, even eccentric. But eccentricity is a valuable characteristic when you remember that the word eccentric means 'off-centre'. These people have a different centre for their lives, a divine focus, which gives them a special freedom. I think of some entrepreneurial believers whose hare-brained schemes used to keep me anxiously on my toes, but who carried the mantle of the 'holy fool' brilliantly – and whose schemes occasionally worked! At other times these special people are somehow the most natural and normal of anyone around them. It's always been a moot question for me whether being a believer is the most natural or the most unnatural thing in the world.

Of course there's a downside to having come under the spell of a special person who has made it possible to believe, or at least to explore the 'something more' of life. The danger is that the idol falls from his or her pinnacle. When a leading figure in any walk of life falls from grace it leaves debris everywhere, and this is particularly the case when that figure is supposed to exemplify the highest ideals of belief or moral judgement. There are many high-profile religious figures who have fallen hard and disillusioned those who had invested heavily in them. It's important, therefore, that such people are understood as 'midwives' of faith and not as objects of faith themselves. When such a story hits the news I always hope that their supporters have developed their own finger-holds on the rock face of faith, sufficient at any rate for them to scramble on to a wide-enough ledge from which they can continue their own climb.

The truth will always be that human beings are fallible, stained by living, carrying wounds that may or may not be deep, but are inevitably damaging. The special people we're thinking about have usually learned how to attend to their wounds, and often have made them the means of healing for others. But if they fail the test of perfection, as they must, neither they nor their Creator is to be blamed. What matters isn't their consistent flawlessness but the direction of their lives. For all of us, the orientation of our lives is the measure of our integrity.

But what is it they are looking towards?

Key question

Is it worth exploring whether what has energized the 'special people' in our lives might also energize us?

To think about

The saint [our 'special person'] is someone who starts a chain reaction of new perception in the world, who reinforces, even among those who don't or can't yet believe, the confidence that there's more to us all than we have suspected. There are some people who so enjoy being who they are that they make everyone else in their vicinity enjoy being themselves – the exact opposite of that more familiar egotism that pushes others into the background so that the star can be centre stage.   Rowan Williams[3]

Story

At the time of the Desert Fathers a magistrate once went into the desert looking for Abba Moses, a man renowned for his piety. He asked someone where he could find this remarkable monk. The man said, 'Don't waste your time. Abba Moses is a heretic and a fraud. He's not any of the things people say he is.' The magistrate went back to the city armed with this knowledge and eager to set the record straight on this supposed paragon of holiness. Someone asked him who it was he had talked to about Abba Moses and was it by any chance a tall black man. 'Well, yes it was actually,' said the magistrate. 'Ah,' the person said. 'That was Abba Moses himself. You met the saint at his best. He'd never make anything of his own sanctity.'

Taking it further

If you feel this line of thinking is worth continuing, here are some things you might do:

1 List your own 'hall of fame' and alongside each name write down what were the qualities in that person that you particularly valued. Think how those qualities have influenced your own way of being and living.

2 Or draw a time line for your life on a largish piece of paper and mark on it the especially significant people who have been part of your journey. What actually was their significance? What motivated them, as far as you could tell? Are there aspects of their lives that you try to emulate?

3 Try writing your own obituary. What would be said of you? What would be picked out as special, and in particular, what aspects of your character would be alluded to? Now try and write the obituary you would like to be written about you. What are the gaps between the two, and how could you bridge the gaps?

4 If you're feeling sufficiently experimental, look in a mirror and ask yourself three questions: How do you see yourself? How do others see you? If there's a God, how does God see you?

15

'Entranced by his company'

The attraction of Jesus

————◆•◆•◆————

'I have a sneaking feeling Jesus got it right.'

'I may not have much time for the Church but Jesus is pretty impressive.'

'I'd like to know more about Jesus, how he lived, and why he died, and if he rose again.'

* * *

The last chapter was about 'special people'. Well, here's one of them – Jesus. He's had more impact on my life than anyone else I can think of. He's the reason I gave up the law, the reason I got ordained, the reason I enjoy the Christian faith so much. But Jesus isn't known in our culture in the way he was some generations ago. One person was asked in a vox pop what he thought of Jesus and the answer came, 'I dunno. Just an ordinary bloke. Don't know that much about him.' Given that 40 per cent of people in a recent survey didn't even realize that Jesus was a historical figure perhaps that response isn't surprising. I have a newspaper advert for Christmas which purports to name all the elements of the festival arrayed on a Christmas tree. There you see words such as joy, parties, presents, food, TV, holidays and lots more – but no mention of Jesus. There's a danger of cultural amnesia as far as Jesus is concerned. And yet, when this figure is allowed to step out of the unopened pages of the Bible, he sometimes strides straight into our hearts. The impact of this man can be revolutionary.

Occasionally our culture lets its guard down and Jesus is portrayed with imagination. Susannah Butler in the *Evening Standard* wrote of the contrast between atheism and a recent film portrayal of Jesus:

> The rich story-telling potential of Bible stories stands in stark contrast to what one observer calls the 'joyless' state of atheism. Could it be that the nature of atheism is responsible for this lean back to the spiritual? *Vice* magazine has picked up on this in an article called, 'Hey, atheists, here's a thought: why don't you stop being dicks? How to make atheism less awful in 2014.' Admittedly, non-believers have a difficult brief – it's a challenge to contend with the greatest story ever told. Atheism offers Richard Dawkins and the worthy Sunday Service, founded in Islington (where else?) and aiming to be 'something like church but without God', while religion has epic drama – floods, plagues and an endless supply of bread. Who would want to make a film about Dawkins when they could have a topless bearded man performing miracles? Just because it's an old story doesn't mean it's not worth retelling. We can only guess what the Big Man Upstairs makes of all this attention. But for now, we must all give thanks for Hot Jesus.[1]

The idea of 'Hot Jesus' may defy our imagination but we all bring our own baggage to our assessment of who he is. Jesus is undeniably an elusive figure. You can't pin him down or write a definitive biography. He slips between our fingers. And yet the Gospels are all about him. The Gospel writers want to focus on him in the way Rembrandt's portraits show a clear central figure while letting the background remain relatively indistinct. Similarly, the Gospel writers don't tell you about the weather or the clothes people wore. And yet the luminous Galilean is in many ways at the centre of world history. Many historical characters have been called 'the Great' – Alexander the Great,

Peter the Great, Catherine the Great, etc. But we never talk about Jesus the Great, because he stands alone; he's 'the only'.

What is it that has attracted countless millions to this penniless preacher from Galilee? He seems to have lived a life of unparalleled beauty, to have taught with astonishing attractiveness, and to have healed whoever love could heal. He died a victim of humanity's scramble for power and fear of goodness; he 'ventured down the dark descent'[2] as the pain of the world funnelled down onto the lonely figure scraped over a cross. But history and faith say that he rose again to vindicate the power of love, and to expose the love of power as bankrupt and corrupt. He rose to give humanity hope that evil was conquered, death was broken-backed and life was irrepressible. The resurrection was truly an event that rippled over the edges of time and into eternity. Malcolm Guite puts it well: 'In a daring and beautiful reversal, God takes the worst we can do to him and turns it into the very best he can do for us.'[3]

I recently spent some weeks with a group of friends on the shores of the Sea of Galilee as we tried to hold together the huge impact of this man with the sheer ordinariness of first-century Galilean life. We visited and loitered in the places where Jesus did these things – taught, healed, debated, but also watched the sun set, chatted about the fishing trade, washed the dishes, laughed at the best jokes, cleaned his teeth, slept in on a day off. This is the man who was in the public eye for less time than it takes these days to get a degree, but whose task in that brief period was to set the world to rights. Here is the man in whom – for many people then, and for colossal numbers now – God once again became visible and audible. This is the human face of God, God's self-portrait. As we pondered these things in the very places where Jesus had grown up and spent most of his short life, we grappled with the paradoxes of a life that many faithful Jews came to admit was both human and divine. They came, within a few short years, to give him the most exalted of titles – 'Son of God', 'Author of life', 'the power and wisdom of God'. But this was the man with whom they had walked the paths of Galilee, gone shopping, and talked about politics and the price of fish. It was astonishing.

This is indeed the figure who, like a great ocean liner, left a massive wake behind him, and did it without any of the communications technology, the special advisers, the media gurus, the syndicated articles, the winsome autobiographies that we would now take for granted. Theologian Jaroslav Pelikan wrote, 'Jesus of Nazareth has been the dominant figure in the history of Western culture for twenty centuries. If it were possible, with some sort of super magnet, to pull up, out of that history, every scrap of metal bearing at least a trace of his name, how much would be left?'[4]

So what kind of response do we make to these grandiose claims? Our sceptical society would like to keep Jesus in a box with other key religious figures; let's not get this out of proportion, we say. Good man, great ideas – but no need to load him with divinity. However, Jesus doesn't let us do that. Unlike other seminal teachers and prophets he unselfconsciously takes on the mantle of God. So, for example, he forgives sins, which only God can do; he rewrites divine law ('But I say to you . . .'); if we are to believe the witnesses ('500 at one time'), he rose from the dead. This is somebody you can't just stuff safely back into the 'great man' box.

There is of course a whole spectrum of ways of describing what the 'divine nature' of Christ means. At one end of that spectrum he is 'one with the Father', fully God and fully human, the second person of the Trinity, God incarnate. At the other end, he was supremely conscious of God's presence in a way no other person has been, and therefore acted in accordance with what he understood to be God's will for his life. There are many positions in between these two. What's more important than precise theological definition, however, is whether we can say, first, that in some remarkable way this man spoke and acted for God, and second, whether we find that, personally and spiritually, we can actually relate to this Jesus today. And these are the steps that no one can persuade any other person to take. We each simply have to ask ourselves, 'What makes most sense here?'

One test of this question is, of course, to read a Gospel and see how Jesus strikes us. Mark is in some ways the freshest Gospel because it's short, punchy and the earliest to be written, probably within 30 or 40 years of Jesus' death. We don't often experience the impact of the story because the Bible is usually given to us in little chunks. So to sit down and read Mark in little more than three-quarters of an hour could be a revealing activity. The actor Robert Powell once had to immerse himself in Mark's Gospel in order to play the part of Jesus. He said, 'I haven't been to church since I was a child and now I have had to smother myself in the Bible. You can read the words but when you come to say them aloud, it's something else. They're electric. What I've read, experienced and played has had a profound effect on me. I've not been converted to the church, but I have been convinced of the divinity of the man.'[5]

I confess that in this chapter I've been more or less assuming that there is a God for Jesus to be related to, a presupposition I've tried not to make in other chapters. For some that might be a step too far. But even here there's some wriggle room. For me at least, the influence of Jesus has been such that I would probably say, if necessary, that I believe in God because Jesus did. That may seem perverse but there are in fact many things which we take on trust because of the person who says them, be it the cosmologist who tells me about the behaviour of the stars or the electrician who tells me not to touch a particular wire. The authenticity of the person himself or herself is what convinces me. Jesus is one such person. I've found his life fascinating, compelling, intriguing, mysterious, scary, captivating, and one I couldn't shake off even if I wanted to. Jesus constantly encourages and confronts me with the clarity of his vision and the resilience of his purpose. His words and actions always seem to have about them the ring of truth, shot through with integrity. He exemplifies compassion around a steel core – both tough-minded and tender-hearted. Put simply, he's taken me closer to God.

But that's only the impact he's made on me. No one can make such a judgement for another. The enigmatic figure of Jesus has to speak for himself. What do you make of this extraordinary teacher/prophet/healer/messiah? Is he worth trusting?

Key question

'Who do you say that I am?' (Mark 8.29)

To think about

Aslan the lion is the Christ-figure in C. S. Lewis's *The Lion, the Witch and the Wardrobe*.

'Is – is he a man?' asked Lucy.

'Aslan a man!' said Mr Beaver sternly. 'Certainly not. I tell you he is the King of the wood and the son of the great Emperor-beyond-the-sea. Don't you know who is the King of Beasts? Aslan is a lion – the Lion, the great Lion.'

'Ooh!' said Susan, 'I'd thought he was a man. Is he – quite safe?'

'Safe?' said Mr Beaver. 'Who said anything about safe? 'Course he isn't safe. But he's good.'[6]

Poem: The Fool and the Hill

The Fool with nowhere to lay his head
came out of nowhere
giving away all he hadn't got
and making people rich, whole,
saved and satisfied,
the Fool who prayed on the hill.

The Fool who came down from the hill
chose a crew of oddballs and
made them into cannon balls
for his salvo of grace,
the Fool who taught on the hill.

The Fool pushed onto the hill
by the people he scandalised in church,
walked calmly down through them and
continued with wisdom,
the Fool on the hill whose time had not yet come.

The Fool transfigured on the hill
co-starred in a 3D Technicolour extravaganza,
the greatest show on earth
about to premiere in Jerusalem,
the Fool who came down from the hill.

The Fool who died on the hill,
betrayed, degraded and deserted,
too foolish in life to disclose his meaning,
a folly confounding this world's wisdom,
the Fool who conquered on the hill.

The Fool who bestrode the hill
In unprecedented glory,
Bestowing his colossal riches
On those who would receive him,
The Fool ascending from the hill
To the Father's eternal glory.   David Grieve[7]

Story

Some years ago broadcaster Gerald Priestland put together a very
popular series on radio called *Priestland's Progress*, in which he set
out to explore what the Christian faith was really about. It was also
the tale of his own pilgrimage of faith. One of the final interviews that

Priestland and his producer recorded was with the nearly blind Bishop of Winchester, John V. Taylor. Priestland asked Taylor what was really happening at Calvary, and the bishop, a gifted theologian with the eye of a poet, embarked on a 14-minute answer to a question that summed up everything that Jesus' life, death and resurrection was about. As the bishop was coming to an end, the producer looked across and saw that Gerald Priestland was crying.

Such is the power of the story.

Taking it further

This chapter might already have gone further than you want to go in the assumptions it's made, but if these are questions you would like to follow up, here are some possibilities:

1 Read a book, such as:

- Tom Wright, *Simply Jesus* (London: SPCK, 2011)
- N. T. Wright and Marcus Borg, *The Meaning of Jesus* (London: SPCK, 1999)
- Philip Yancey, *The Jesus I Never Knew* (London: HarperCollins, 1995)
- John Pritchard, *Living Jesus* (London: SPCK, 2010)

2 Better still, read a Gospel: Mark for hard-hitting narrative, Matthew for teaching against a Jewish background, Luke for a focus on women, healing and people on the margins, John for profound reflection on the significance of Jesus. Try to read the chosen Gospel in large chunks so that you get the flow of the narrative and its underlying meaning. If you then want to go further you might start looking at Tom Wright's 'New Testament for Everyone' series.

3 Ask yourself what you think Jesus was really like, filling out for yourself the descriptions of what he said and did in the Gospels. And see how you respond to this description:

> I looked at the gospel again and quite suddenly a new portrait seemed to stare at me out of the pages. I had

never previously thought of a laughing, joking Jesus, physically strong and active, fond of good company and a glass of wine, telling funny stories, using, as every good teacher does, paradox and imagination . . . applying nicknames to his friends and holding his companions spellbound with his talk . . . As I reflected on this I came to the conclusion that we should have been absolutely entranced by his company.

Lord Hailsham, *The Door Wherein I Went*[8]

4 If you dare, take a story from a Gospel (I recommend the healing of the paralysed man in Luke 5.17–26) and try to imagine yourself in that little house, watching what was happening. Let the story unfold slowly, sit in there with the crowd, feel the crush, look at the weather-beaten faces around you and the rough material of their clothes, watch what's going on, listen to the voice of Jesus. Follow the whole story through and then watch Jesus after the event – you might even talk to him. What do you make of all that's happened? What did you make of Jesus? Only when you're ready, come out of the little house and reflect on what it meant.

16

'Who speaks for the poor?'

The search for justice and social engagement

------•◆•------

'This inequality really gets to me.'

'I want to give everything for everything rather than nothing for nothing.'

'The world can't go on like this.'

* * *

Holy Trinity Church on Clapham Common is where William Wilberforce and his fellow members of the Clapham Sect found the spiritual strength to campaign for social change in nineteenth-century Britain, including the abolition of slavery. There is in the church an old, well-worn table on which Wilberforce wrote the anti-slavery act – and on which Holy Communion is still celebrated every week. That's the authentic voice of Christianity, combining secular and sacred in a way that should never have been divorced. Healthy religion is always concerned with changing society in the direction of justice, compassion and mercy. People of faith should always be involved in bandaging the bruised and picking up the broken, but they should also be asking the questions, 'Why are they bruised? What made them broken?' And that places us in the field of change.

To some sceptics this vision of what faith means is attractive enough to encourage them to associate with a faith community, not because they share the faith but because they want to contribute to the well-being of the wider community. We all need allies when we undertake a major task or want to work towards our ideals, and if we are to look around society today and ask where the vision for change is most likely to come from, there are few candidates with the pedigree of the faith communities. There are of course hundreds of caring organizations that are not faith-based, and millions of caring members of the community who are not motivated by faith but by sheer goodness and generosity. But loving your neighbour, loving your enemy, caring for the stranger, etc., is written into the title deeds of the Christian faith, and so if you are inclined to look in the churches you will certainly find like minds on the importance of practical compassion and the search for justice.

There are 30,000 faith-based charities in Britain.[1] They range from the big players such as Christian Aid, the Children's Society, World Vision and CAFOD to the almshouses and local charities that oil the wheels of small communities. Over 80 per cent of churches are involved in some way with food banks; many participate in street pastor schemes and work with the homeless. A church I know in Abingdon does both of these things but also runs a debt counselling service, works in prisons and with ex-offenders, offers lunches for the elderly, helps families from overseas to find their feet, and runs a smart coffee shop for anyone in the local community. And of course behind the institutional social action of all these churches are the million acts of kindness and love which daily sustain and develop our social fabric.

There's a larger backdrop to all this community-building activity. Lord Glasman, the founder of the 'Blue Labour' movement, argues that both the market and the state have failed in creating a just society dedicated to the common good. Rather, it's faith groups that hold the key to building a new society based on participation, relationship, solidarity and vocation.[2] He challenges faith communities to live up to their calling and to go into battle for the poor with the energy and conviction that the title deeds of their faith demand. If the Church had not got caught up with internal dissension on second-order

issues, this could be an attractive manifesto for the many ideal-
ists who find themselves without a home.

Pope Francis' 2015 encyclical on the environment, for example,
found many allies who didn't share all the tenets of his faith but
who responded to the vision he offered that our relationship
to the natural world needs to be based on love and not the
accountants' bottom line. We care for creation because we love
the natural world, and this approach to the well-worn arguments
on the environment and climate change significantly raises the
quality of debate. George Monbiot wrote in *The Guardian*,
'Acknowledging our love for the living world does something
that a library full of papers on sustainable development and
ecosystem services cannot; it engages the imagination as well
as the intellect. It inspires belief; and this is essential to the
lasting success of any movement.'[3] We don't live 'on' this earth
but 'in' it, so everything we do affects everything there is, and
this is where our ultimate values show up.

The introduction of that word 'love' is an interesting move.
It suggests a frustration with the myopic vision of a society that
has based its future on microchips. The possibilities of robotics
are both exciting and terrifying but they inevitably omit the most
important characteristic of humanity, which is the capacity to
love. In his book *Arctic Dreams*, Barry Lopez writes:

> The conventional wisdom of our time is that European
> man has advanced by enormous strides since the age of
> cathedrals. He has landed on the moon. He has cured
> smallpox. He has harnessed the power of the atom. Another
> argument, however, might be made in the opposite direc-
> tion, that all European man has accomplished in 900 years
> is a more complicated manipulation of materials, a more
> astounding display of his grasp of the physical principles
> of matter. That we are dazzled by mere styles of expression.
> That ours is not an age of mystics but of singular adepts,
> of performers. That the erection of the cathedrals was the

last wild stride European man made before falling back into the confines of his intellect ... There is one word from the time of the cathedrals: *agape*, an expression of intense spiritual affinity with the mystery that is sharing life with other life ...[4]

Faith communities can change the discourse on social justice. They may be worth joining.

Or not, of course. Because there are also church communities that are irreparably and depressingly in-turned. Sometimes this is because they've never quite grasped the social implications of the gospel. Sometimes it's because they haven't got beyond the 'holy club' mentality of a group of people meeting for their own enjoyment. And sometimes it's because the church is small, the members elderly and the capacity just isn't there – although you might find among them some giants of prayer holding the community and wider world before God week in, week out. Nevertheless, the sympathetic inquirer with a social conscience is entitled to expect some significant elements of a gospel that is good news for the poor, proclaims release to the captives and recovery of sight for the blind, and lets the oppressed go free (from Luke 4.18). Or at its simplest, a church that loves its neighbour, near and far.

I have long found it intolerable that so many people still die of hunger on a planet of plenty, but at least I know that my puny contribution to righting that wrong is allied to that of a huge number of other people similarly outraged, and that our motivation is something to do with love. That love is not restricted by national borders. The Bible says just once that we are to love our neighbours as ourselves, but it says 36 times that we should 'love the stranger'. Such a conviction must surely change the way we approach the issue of immigration and asylum.

Then again, how can it be right that one per cent of the world's population owns more than half the world's wealth?

How can it be right that top CEOs in Britain have annual packages of nearly £5 million, a figure 183 times greater than average earnings? How can it be acceptable that 85 people own more than the 3.5 billion poorest people on the planet put together? This isn't necessarily to blame the one per cent, the top CEOs or the 85 wealthiest people; it's to shame the global systems that allow such poverty and inequality to exist. So we protest, many of us, and lest we feel impotent in the face of such enormity we may remember the words of the anthropologist Margaret Mead, who said, 'Never doubt that a small group of thoughtful, committed citizens can change the world; indeed they're the only ones who ever have.'[5]

Believers have always been in the forefront of such 'small groups'. I remember the stunts we got up to in Taunton when I was a vicar and we had 'rich world – poor world' meals, giant snakes and ladders illustrating global inequality, week-long fasts by people living in a shack on the high street, the sale of mini-loaves in Christian Aid week – all in our attempt to raise awareness of the inequalities pervading our world. Self-righteous? Maybe. Well-intentioned? Certainly. But the important point here is that we found ourselves attracting many people who would not otherwise have considered a faith community a likely partner in their political engagement.

When Barack Obama arrived in Chicago as a young community organizer he joined a church because his boss told him that was the place to go if he wanted to help the poor. 'The churches are the only game in town,' he said. 'That's where the people are, and that's where the values are, even if they've been buried under a lot of bullshit.'[6] (Point noted.) Martin Luther King used to contend that Christians needed to be 'creatively maladjusted' to society's attitudes and values, and it's a similar stance of 'critical friendship' that the faith communities need to have with governments, of whatever flavour. Mrs Thatcher may have been irritated by the Church of England's report on urban Britain, *Faith in the City*, or by the Archbishop's sermon after the Falklands war, or the Bishop of Durham's criticisms of government during the miners' strike, but the Church was providing the only effective prophetic voice at that time and it won many friends. Charles Clarke, Home Secretary from 2004 to 2006 and an agnostic, remarked that his experience working in inner-city Hackney in the early 1980s showed him that 'almost every leader of the voluntary, community and charitable organizations which promoted education, social care and community strength, did it because of their own committed religious faith'.[7]

My father was the vicar of a large parish in Blackpool. He worked very hard for not much money, which was one of the reasons I said I would never be ordained. But he loved it. He was involved in setting up a branch of the Samaritans in the town and would regularly complete a long working day with an evening on duty on the phone. I remember him and my mother scrubbing thoroughly a recently purchased house destined to be an Abbeyfield home for the elderly (how much actual scrubbing my father did is not known). The lives of some of his 40,000 parishioners always seemed to be breaking into our family life with pastoral crises or practical problems. Children's, youth and schools work abounded, along with much involvement in civic affairs to benefit the community. It was a sacrificial life, but one that gave my father great satisfaction as he tried to follow his Master by loving his neighbour, especially his neighbour in need, and even loving his enemy – if he'd had any.

Love always has the last word.

Key question

What could you bring to the local church as it tries to make a difference in the community?

To think about

When he taught students at his ashram in India, Gandhi spoke of seven deadly sins:

1 Politics without principle
2 Wealth without work
3 Commerce without morality
4 Pleasure without conscience
5 Education without character
6 Science without humanity
7 Worship without sacrifice.

Story

The church was at a low ebb. A new rector came but not much changed. There was a home for people with learning difficulties next door to the church but the church hadn't had anything to do with it, until one Sunday morning during the main service, a man from the home took off all his clothes. Someone in the congregation took off her shawl, put it round him and took him to the church's ancillary rooms. The church community had been awakened to the needs of the home next door and from that time on began to serve the people there, in a variety of ways. And so the church grew, as people were drawn in to this new ministry.

Taking it further

If these issues ring any bells, you might like to think about some of the following courses of action:

1 Get involved! Take the plunge. Ask a priest or minister who you should talk to about your particular passion for social justice. Risk the occasional dispiriting encounter with someone whose views are completely off the wall (doesn't every human group have them?) and see what you can offer in terms of particular expertise or simple enthusiasm. You don't

have to buy the whole package; churches are meant to be porous communities of truth-seekers and apprentice believers. No one has it all sussed, and what you bring is unique. A woman once said she was leaving the church because it wasn't speaking out about animal rights. The vicar replied, 'If you leave you're right, it won't. *You're* the church speaking out on animal rights.' Every contribution matters because every person has gifts.

2 Use the internet to see what voluntary groups are operating in the community, and see if there's one that coincides with your commitments. It may have its base in a faith community, or it may have many believers deeply involved in its current work. Then join in! It's widely acknowledged that if you took away the believers from the charities and community groups in society, many of them would collapse. Research shows that people of faith are strongly committed to the well-being of their communities and are more likely than others to be involved in voluntary organizations, often in leadership.[8]

3 Read some of the passages that express the biblical mandate for believers being involved in issues of justice and peace. There are hundreds, but here are a few:

- Isaiah 58; Amos 5.21–24; Micah 6.6–8
- Matthew 5.1–14, 43–48; 25.31–46
- Luke 4.16–21.

4 As the T-shirt says, 'Just do it.'

17

'Let it be'

Letting go and being surprised

———•◆•———

'If you're there, God, show me.'

'OK, let's give it a try.'

'God came right out of the blue.'

* * *

There was once a cartoon in the *New Yorker* magazine which showed two men at their desks. One says to the other, 'By God, for a moment there it all made sense.' There are times when it feels as if we've broken through, 'got it', when the lottery balls all fall into place. Whatever it is we've been puzzling about suddenly makes sense, the mist clears and the confusions in our thinking suddenly resolve like those Magic Eye pictures of a few years ago. There are a multitude of paths to faith, but in terms of this breakthrough moment, there are at least two well-known routes. One is a decision to let go of the objections and barriers to belief which have lain across the road so stubbornly and so long. The other is to be hijacked by some experience that comes out of the blue and changes the game entirely. As someone said to me once of such an experience, 'Nothing happened and everything changed.'

Let's look at that first route, the decision to let go. It may be the case that we have argued with God or with ourselves or with some poor victimized friend for long enough and we realize that arguing will only get us so far. Perhaps we've finally come to accept that intellectual knowledge needs to be complemented by personal or relational knowledge. Not every-thing can be described adequately by reducing it to equations and biochemical reactions. When asked to describe a girlfriend, a man might produce an impressive list of attributes and achievements; if he is particularly gifted he might even be able to recall her height, the cut of her hair and the colour of her eyes. But the fullest description of all comes when he says, 'She's wonderful, and I love her.' Personal or relational language is different from scientific language but it's none the worse for that, just as the language of the poet or philosopher is just as valid as that of the mathematician or physicist. Sometimes, therefore, the analytical left brain needs to rein itself in and let the intuitive right brain have a go.

The Christian writer C. S. Lewis had had a running battle with his intellect for years on the subject of religious belief. He remembered being given, while on the top of a bus going up Headington Hill in Oxford, a choice which felt like being allowed, if he wanted, to take off the armour that encased him. There was no pressure, neither threat nor promise, but he knew the implications were incalculable. He unbuckled the armour. But that didn't mean he had become a believer, just that 'I felt as if I were a man of snow at long last beginning to melt.'[1] He goes on, in his autobiography *Surprised by Joy*, 'Really, a young atheist cannot guard his faith too carefully,' because some time later he finally gave up his resistance to the hound of heaven.

> You must picture me alone in that room at Magdalen, night after night, feeling, whenever my mind lifted even for a second from my work, the steady, unrelenting approach of him whom I so earnestly desired not to meet. That which I greatly feared had at last come upon me. In the Trinity term of 1929 I gave in, and admitted that God was God, and knelt and prayed: perhaps, that night, the most dejected and reluctant convert in all England. I did not

> then see what is now the most shining and obvious thing;
> the Divine humility which will accept a convert even on
> such terms.[2]

This is a classic account of 'letting go', ceasing to resist, and
it might ring bells with some who long ago waved God down
and took him in for questioning, but have never before sought
a conviction. Now at last the arrest is made, though it may not
be clear who has arrested whom. Now at last there is 'conviction', however reluctant it may be.

A man I know could take you to the gate where his defining
moment took place. As he came through that gate into the
field beyond he finally said to himself, and to whatever he
then understood of God, 'That's it; I'm in.' Another man with
a colourful past had played on the edges of faith for some
months. The image which finally helped him was that of
'stepping over the line'. He had come thus far; the arguments
were becoming circular; here was the line that he could step
over; was that what he wanted to do? He decided he did, and
with it came a rush of freedom. These were only the first steps,
of course. When you cross a national border the countryside
doesn't look very different until you've travelled much further
into the new country. Gradually you come to realize you're now
in a new land where the customs and the language, as well as
the landscape, have changed considerably.

This was my experience at university where I began the task
of growing up and finding a shape and direction for my life.
A course in law was useful – being fair, weighing evidence,
looking for weaknesses in arguments – but eventually I realized
it was up to me to decide what I wanted to do with the accumu-
lated information I now had. I decided to cross the border.
Equally of course it was important that I didn't leave my brain
at border control, or I would arrive in the new territory half-
dressed and limping. The legal training has never left me and
I often go back to the frontier to argue with the border guards

on both sides. The philosopher Kierkegaard spoke of the leap of faith, but he didn't mean by that a leap in the dark into the irrational; he meant that religion can only give meaning to life in a penultimate way, it can only go so far. In order to get over the abyss of meaninglessness you need to take the leap of faith into the embrace of God himself, not the human constructs we put around God. This is 'letting go'.

The other route to moments of spiritual disclosure, when it all suddenly seems to make sense, is the experience of surprise. 'God' drops a ladder down in the middle of washing up, bathing the children, walking the dog, indeed anywhere. These are given moments, uninvited, unpredictable, pure grace. Something happens that upends our world-view and we have to begin again. I have a friend whose unlikely career had included being a Bunny girl, a Covent Garden opera singer and a children's TV presenter. She was eating roasted cauliflower in a Hari Krishna tent at a Body, Mind and Spirit fair when she clearly felt hands on her shoulder and heard the words 'Follow me'. She knew who it was at once, and next day went to communion in a local church. She's now ordained.

There's no groundwork you can do for this kind of experience and no easy way of analysing it. Why this person? Why now? Why this way? These questions won't advance the stock of human understanding very far. There are times when we simply have to admit that life is drenched in mystery and the richer for it. Predictability isn't a divine attribute. But surprise reflects the open texture of a quantum universe (see Chapter 11), so when God arrives we have to hope we've left the door ajar. Again, let's be sceptical about our scepticism.

The common factor in these epiphanies is the sudden unexpectedness of them. They can occur when eating roasted cauliflower in a Hari Krishna tent, or in a space capsule returning from the moon. Edgar Mitchell was an astronaut on Apollo 14 and from his tiny capsule 'he saw planet earth floating freely in the vastness of space and was captivated by a profound sense of universal connectedness. He later said, "The presence of divinity became almost palpable, and I knew that life in the universe was not just an accident based on random processes."' Then, crucially, he said, 'The knowledge came to me directly.'[3] He hadn't set himself up for this gifted moment. It just came, almost literally, out of the blue.

Most experiences of transcendence are less esoteric than this. They occur in the midst of everyday life but are rarely written up for fear of polite ridicule. Nevertheless, experiences of the 'beyond in the everyday' are too common to be dismissed. Academic studies such as those of the Scientific and Medical Network in England, the Institute of Noetic Sciences in California, and research conducted under the auspices of the John Templeton Foundation, consistently find that surprisingly large percentages of the population have had epiphany-like moments.[4] David Hay, when Reader in Spiritual Education at Nottingham University, quoted research which indicated that those reporting 'spiritual experience' went up from 48 per cent of the UK population in 1987 to 75 per cent in 2000. Fifty-five per cent acknowledged an emerging transcendent meaning in their lives and 38 per cent claimed an experience of God.[5] Public moods in religion and spirituality, and how people speak of them, change quickly at the present time, so it would be unwise to build too much on precise figures, but the general outcome is clear – a large proportion of the UK population have had spiritual or numinous experiences. They aren't weird. The question is how we evaluate them.

The spiritual journey can start by letting go at last of the arguments and resistances that have kept this dimension of life in a box with a warning that the contents may seriously damage your health. Equally, it may start with the unpredictable eruption into our lives of some experience of the spiritual/divine that we didn't seek but can't deny. Either way the onus is back on us. What will we do now?

Key question

Have I resisted long enough?

Poem: Pax

All that matters is to be at one with the living God
to be a creature in the house of the God of Life.

Like a cat asleep on a chair
at peace, in peace
and at one with the master of the house, with the mistress,
at home, at home in the house of the living,
sleeping on the hearth, and yawning before the fire.

Sleeping on the hearth of the living world,
yawning at home before the fire of life
feeling the presence of the living God
like a great reassurance
a deep calm in the heart
a presence
as of a master sitting at the board
in his own and greater being,
in the house of life.   D. H. Lawrence[6]

Taking it further

If you'd like to explore the ideas in this chapter further, here
are some ways you might begin:

1 Find a Christian friend (or one of the clergy you could relate
  to) and ask that person if she or he has had an experience
  of 'letting go', or an unexpected awareness of God that came
  out of the blue. Mull over the answers and ask follow-up
  questions. Perhaps be open to the same happening to you!

2 Get hold of one or two of the books mentioned at the end of Chapter 12, or:

- Brian McLaren, *Finding Faith* (Grand Rapids: Zondervan, 1999)
- Rob Bell, *What We Talk About When We Talk About God* (London: HarperCollins, 2013).

3 Find a church with a beginners' group of some kind where you can ask questions and discuss what all this might mean. Look out for Pilgrim and Alpha courses. Church websites can tell you a lot about the character and tone of different churches and whether they'll be environments which are conducive to your way of thinking and your kind of interests.

18

'So what?'

The beyond in the everyday

———◆•◆•◆———

'I'm interested in spirituality but it all seems a bit of a jumble.'

'I think there's something in all this spirituality stuff but I'm not sure what to do next.'

* * *

When I taught practical theology at a college in Durham we had a retired bishop helping out at our Urban Study Centre. At the end of a student's account of some significant experience in Gateshead, our bishop would say, somewhat gruffly, 'So what?' It was said as a challenge, and it was the vital question. So what does all that mean? So what are you going to do with that? So what significance does that have for ministry? I still ask myself that question when I'm trying to make sense of a new experience. 'So what was all that about?' And it's where we're left at the end of this book, in which we've been looking at different human responses to life events and the possibility that they may point beyond themselves to something more. 'So what?' What now?

This 'something more' is the subject matter of spirituality, which you might remember in Rowan Williams's definition is 'the cultivation of a sensitive and rewarding relationship with eternal truth and love'.[1] Note the outward-facing nature of that definition. It's far removed from the self-absorption of some understandings of spirituality, what Julie Burchill describes as 'seeking yet another way to pamper oneself once the effects of the Rainforest

Ritual body-wrap have worn off'.[2] It's the seriously fascinating business of exploring the nature of reality and our relationship with it.

On the matrix of 'known knowns' and 'unknown unknowns',
the question of God/the Beyond/the Absolute must be a known
unknown. We know that we can't know for certain. To think
otherwise would be rather like thinking that Hamlet could be
certain about Shakespeare, when clearly Hamlet inhabits a
different order of existence from his author. In a university
sermon the writer Howard Jacobson said, 'However you explain
it, I like the idea, whenever I encounter it, of a God forever out
of reach. Whoever tells me that my failure to reach him proves
his non-existence has merely closed his mind to my ongoing
curiosity.'[3] We should expect any self-respecting Transcendence
to be beyond our understanding.

We are inevitably going to fail if we seek to put this mystery
on the dissecting table. The key issue about mystery, indeed, is
whether we see it as something to resolve or something to
deepen. On the one hand there are those who are clear about
their knowledge of God and want to dispel any mystery, like a
'God correspondent' laying out the facts. On the other hand
there are those who aren't comfortable with black and white
answers and prefer to explore ambiguity, to admit they don't
know, to come at the mystery crabwise. This latter approach is
concerned to deepen the mystery at the heart of spirituality
and to relish the spiritual journey to the centre of our lives. Or,
to use the image of Mike Riddell, 'It's better to be sitting by the
fire inside a building where the walls don't quite meet than to
be outside in the cold complaining about the lack of symmetry.'[4]

To claim to understand the divine is to diminish it. Our language about God is often too distressed and tired for the task. If
believers continue to roll out improbable, broken language about
God, God will increasingly seem to belong to another age, small,
irrelevant and mean. And if the content of that language speaks
of God like an all-controlling magician, believers will come across
as intellectually moribund and left behind in the arena of ideas.

The concept of God as located somewhere else, doing something else, and occasionally dropping in to disturb events in the visible world, has many disadvantages, not the least of which is that it makes God optional. Belief in a God of those limited characteristics is bound to be a 'take it or leave it' issue, whereas one of the themes of this book is that any viable concept of the divine must be all-inclusive – everything else is contingent but God is not contingent. The universe, existence, you and I, etc., could not just carry on without God. In this understanding of God, God is not simply an option, but a necessity.

This God of Everything has to be the foundational Reality for the entire mystery of creation – a universe of which 96 per cent is unknown because it consists of black holes, a universe whose 'edge' is roughly ninety billion trillion miles away. This Beyond/Absolute isn't a domestic deity answering to our whims. The trouble is, the God who forms the very basis of existence is heavily camouflaged in the breathtaking complexity of the universe; how else could such fundamental energy be envisaged? Greater clarity would overwhelm us. But in terms of God's 'existence' (a very misleading word), absence of evidence is not evidence of absence. The conviction I'm offering is that *everything* is saturated in divine possibility.

You see what I mean about language not being up to the task! The poet-philosopher Rumi said wisely, 'Sell your cleverness and buy bewilderment.' Nevertheless, words and silence are all we have. Silence is a particularly valuable language to use about God. At the end of his conversation with God, Job says of God, 'I have uttered what I did not understand, things too wonderful for me, which I did not know' (Job 42.3). It's right that we should be reduced to the humility and riches of silence, because at this point the half-gods leave and God can arrive. The language of silence has been that favoured by the strong mystical tradition that has bound together Christian spirituality and the spirituality of other faiths. It embraces the mute, halting attempts of humanity to comprehend the transcendent without the embarrassment of seeming to use nursery language in the setting of a university. It also puts humans in 'receive' mode instead of incessant 'transmit'.

The contrast in perceptions of the divine comes out clearly in a conversation in Sarah Winman's novel *When God was a Rabbit*. The narrator is talking to an old family friend:

> 'Do you believe in God, Arthur?' I said, eating the last piece of sponge.
>
> 'Do I believe in an old man in the clouds with a white beard judging us mortals with a moral code of one to ten? Good Lord no, my sweet Elly, I do not! I would have been cast out from this life years ago with my tatty history. Do I believe in a mystery; the unexplained phenomenon that is life itself? The greater something that illuminates inconsequence in our lives; that gives us something to strive for as well as the humility to brush ourselves down and start all over again? Then yes, I do. It is the source of art, of beauty, of love, and proffers the ultimate goodness to mankind. That to me is God. That to me is life. That is what I believe in.[5]

Here's a description of some subtlety, looking for an understanding of the divine that encompasses life, purpose, art, love and more. Nevertheless we struggle to find words adequate to the task of speaking about God. If we rightly have to let go of images that sound like an All-controlling Magician, or an Unaccountable Despot, where shall we find metaphors today that bear some of the weight we need? We may talk of the Infinite Sustainer, or the Inexhaustible Presence, or Being-Itself, but every time we come up with a new arrangement of words it feels as if we're playing for time or indulging our own subjectivity.

However, one thing that is undoubtedly necessary for a viable approach to the mystery of God is that it embraces the dark experiences of life. 'Cheap religion denies the darkness. True religion steps right into it,' says Richard Rohr.[6] Cheery optimism that

God will protect believers from bad times should have died in the stubborn witness of a child's grave or the perennial carnage of war. Yet there remain many people who convince themselves that faith gives a second layer of protection against disaster, that somehow their faith will make them immune from things going wrong. More realistic is the courage of the family in Michael Rosen's children's book *We're Going on a Bear Hunt*. The family sets off hopefully, saying together, 'We're going on a bear hunt. We're going to catch a big one. What a beautiful day! We're not scared.' On the way they encounter a variety of obstacles, and each time there's a repeated refrain, 'We can't go over it. We can't go under it. Oh no! We've got to go through it!'[7] Faith gives us the resources to go *through* the mud and mayhem we sometimes find ourselves in, not to avoid them. No credible version of the transcendent can hope to be convincing today that doesn't incorporate a way of living with the tragic dimension of life.

In Chapter 7 I tried to point out how all the great faith traditions are founded on the obstinate facts of human suffering and evil. This is why there is an ultimate seriousness about spirituality, far removed from the understanding of spirituality as self-help therapy. And in this arena of serious spirituality the image of a suffering messiah has lasting power. The cross is a point of reference for many people who find themselves clinging to the wreckage in the open sea of life's misfortunes. And behind that iconic figure of the crucified carpenter is the unique gift of Christianity – the disclosure of divine mystery in the only language humankind could grasp, in other words a human life. How else could the blistering reality of God be comprehended by mere human minds? Jesus transformed the staggeringly high voltage of divinity to manageable proportions. Certainly there is an affront to common sense in God inhabiting humanity – theologians call it 'the scandal of particularity' – but that's the genius of Christianity.

The premise of this book is that God keeps leaking into our lives in spite of our unfortunate failure to notice. We lack the language to describe the experience of 'something more' which so often lies beyond, through or on the far side of these moments. The older discourse of faith no longer works and a new one has not yet been devised. Perhaps, therefore, we might return to the image behind the struggling words, the image of a particular man, the image of God.

'The Word became flesh and lived among us, and we have seen his glory' (John 1.14).

Could this be the key 'scent' that God has laid down? Perhaps the old songs are still the best.

Key question

So what?

Poem: Love

LOVE bade me welcome; yet my soul drew back,
    Guilty of dust and sin.
But quick-eyed Love, observing me grow slack
    From my first entrance in,
Drew nearer to me, sweetly questioning
    If I lack'd anything.

'A guest,' I answer'd, 'worthy to be here:'
    Love said, 'You shall be he.'
'I, the unkind, ungrateful? Ah, my dear,
    I cannot look on Thee.'
Love took my hand and smiling did reply,
    'Who made the eyes but I?'

'Truth, Lord; but I have marr'd them: let my shame
    Go where it doth deserve.'
'And know you not,' says Love, 'Who bore the blame?'
    'My dear, then I will serve.'
'You must sit down,' says Love, 'and taste my meat.'
    So I did sit and eat.   George Herbert[8]

To think about

The fact that we question is also part of the answer. If our soul revolts at the bitterness, the strife, the malevolence we see about us, what are we asking questions about if we think there is no sense in anything? ... I do not believe in an uncaring deity. I do not believe in an irrational universe. I believe in goodness, truthfulness, loving kindness, beauty, generosity, loyalty. They all exist and they are all qualities which demand just as much explanation as malevolence, cruelty, ugliness, meanness and treachery ... As I approach the throne of the ineffable, the more mere words fail to express my inmost feelings, and I take refuge in metaphor, in poetry, in music, in admiration for beauty in a landscape, in a sunset, in the plumage of a bird or a butterfly, in the works of man, in stone, in colour, in sound. But my doubts finally dissolve in wonder, in longing, in adoration. And, lo, a paradox appears. I seek God, and behold a bedraggled human figure impaled for public ridicule upon a gibbet. I despair of man, and behold the same figure, enthroned in majesty above the clouds. If I go up to heaven He is there. If I descend to the depths of misery and grief, He is there also. He is Alpha and Omega, the source of my being and the end of my pilgrimage. He is love, at once the beloved and the eternal lover ... He is always present and yet constantly eludes my grasp. Being infinite, he cannot be comprised in my understanding. Remaining Christian, I am constantly reassured in my wandering, in my doubting, and as constantly led back by my trusting. I do not know. I do not pretend to know. But I trust, and therefore I believe.

Lord Hailsham, *A Sparrow's Flight*[9]

Taking it further

Faith is taking the first step, even when you can't see the whole staircase.   Martin Luther King

Questions for group discussion

———•◆•———

Groups might find that some of the material in the 'Taking it further' section of each chapter provides stimulus to discussion. It would be worth looking at that first and identifying helpful starters there, and then looking at the following questions.

One possible way of structuring the sessions would be as follows:

- **Introduction** from one member of the group, either describing the content of the chapter or reminding the group of it if they've read it.
- **Snaps.** Immediate responses from members of the group describing where their experience echoed material in the chapter.
- **Study.** Discussion of the questions culled from 'Taking it further' and the relevant questions below.
- **Spin-offs.** What further action might result from the discussion either for individuals or the church.
- **Go again.** Given that there are 17 chapters in the book, you might want to take two at a group meeting.

1 'Is there more to life than meets the eye?'

This is an introductory chapter and so does not have a distinct set of questions, although it can still be discussed.

2 'Is that it?'

- Do you remember a time before faith was real to you (maybe that's where you are now)? Was there a feeling of incompleteness or dissatisfaction or something like it? (There doesn't need to have been!) How would you describe that feeling? What did you do with it?

- What is it all for, this life? Is it possible to say without seeming trite?
- What difference does a faith make to the experience of life? (Playwright Dennis Potter said that religion wasn't the bandage but the wound . . .)
- How would you like to be remembered? You might write a brief inscription for a gravestone. What stops you from being that kind of person?

3 'All you could desire'

- Bertrand Russell wrote of 'searching for something transfigured and infinite'. Do you recognize a longing for God in yourself? Why might it be 'a terrible pain' as Russell said?
- Are there aspects of life and of faith that you long for now?
- What would you say to someone who was longing for an encounter with God?
- Does Psalm 139 feel reassuring or slightly unsettling?

4 'Life couldn't hold any more'

- When have you felt most fully alive? Did those occasions have religious significance, either then or later?
- Have you known that kind of transfiguring experience that Thomas Merton, Roger Bannister and Barbara Ehrenreich had? Does it matter if you haven't? What would be the nearest you've come to such an experience?
- What aspect of your faith or belief system brings you most 'life'?
- Are these experiences of 'life in all its fullness' ones you can create or do they, of necessity, have to come as gifts?

5 'Earth's crammed with heaven'

- Share your most breathtaking experiences. Are they all to do with nature? Why?

- Are these experiences of wonder inevitably somewhat senti-mental and 'middle class'? Where might wonder be found in, say, tough urban conditions?
- If you know the book of Job, how does it leave you feeling? What do you make of God's answer in chapters 38 and 39, and what do you think of the blessings Job gets at the very end?
- If you're feeling adventurous, try to compose a group psalm of praise (in modern language), each person adding a line.

6 'Nobody's perfect'

- Is anyone prepared to speak about a time when life had become very messy and what they did about it, or how it was resolved? If so, how did faith help, or didn't it?
- 'That's how the light gets in.' Has it been your experience that when 'the crack' appears in your life, light has come in as well?
- Why does God allow the world to get in such a mess? (Huge question!)
- How could your church improve the way it stands with, and if possible helps, those whose lives have got in a mess?

7 'Hell and high water'

- What have you learned through suffering or by being close to someone suffering?
- What was the place of prayer in the face of that suffering? Was it possible, helpful, 'effective', 'ineffective'?
- The chapter looked at the emotional, spiritual and intellectual aspects of suffering. What's your response to those thoughts? Did you find yourself agreeing, disagreeing, questioning?
- Some psalms are cries of despair and anger in the face of suffering. Psalm 88 is an extreme example because it doesn't end in praise as so many do. How do we square the experi-ence behind that psalm, and our own raw experience, with Paul's confident assertion that 'all things work together for good for those who love God' (Romans 8.28)?

8 'Don't just do something, sit there'

- How easy do you find it to be still and silent? What is your experience of it? What gets in the way, and what helps you?
- How important is it as a society that we lower the level of noise both inside and outside ourselves? Is this desire for more stillness mainly felt by introverts?
- In 1 Kings 19, Elijah experiences God not in the wind, the earthquake or the fire, but in the 'still, small voice'. What is the significance of this for Elijah and for us?
- Put together as many endings as you can to the phrase 'Be still and . . .', e.g.: 'Be still and hear the birds sing', 'Be still and let God order your thoughts.'

9 'Tell it slant'

- Think of a painting, piece of music, poem or book which opens up a spiritual door to you. Describe it to the group and explain its effect on you.
- Has great architecture or any film had the same effect on you? If so, describe it as above.
- Have any works of art, music, etc., had the opposite effect on you and closed down spiritual interpretation? Can art be 'demonic' as well as divine?
- Are there ways in which your church could use the arts more in worship, learning or evangelism?

10 'Coming home'

- How important and effective were your first experiences of 'place', hospitality and community when you started to take the Christian faith seriously?
- How can you balance the numinous and the personal, 'the vertical and the horizontal', in a church's life and worship?
- Go through the 'Tips for church leaders' from Linda Woodhead and discuss their significance. How would you put each one into practice in your church?

- If there are fewer churches in future and more meeting in informal, more functional, settings, how significant will that be?

11 'Why is there something rather than nothing?'

- Do you ever come up against these questions of science and religion? How and where? Do you feel equipped to engage with them?
- People sometimes use the word 'myth' to mean something that isn't true. Christians and others use the word to mean something that is always true. So how does the 'myth' of the creation story (or stories) of Genesis 1—3 work today, i.e. what are its value and meanings for us?
- How do you regard the miracles recorded in the New Testament in the light of modern science? If something has a scientific explanation can it still have a spiritual meaning, and if so can you give an example?
- We say something is 'a miracle of modern science'. You could think of examples. What part does God play in them?

12 'Darkness at noon'

- Have you experienced this kind of nightmare? How did you cope with it? Was your faith relevant at that time?
- Theologian Charles Ringma wrote: 'The safest place in all the world is to be sheltered in the love of God.' Who might that help and when, or is it too twee?
- Imagine a non-believing friend has just had very bad medical news. What might you do and say?
- The disciples' world collapsed one evening in a garden after dinner. Use your imagination to think what they might have thought and felt then and where they might have gone. What do you think they did between then and when we catch up with them again on Easter day?

13 'Hatching, matching, dispatching'

- What impact have any of the 'occasional offices' of baptism, marriage and funerals had on you? Were any particularly significant, and if so, why?
- Imagine you are a Christian asked out for a drink by a friend wanting to know about your faith. In the group, share the answers you might give to the friend's questions: How did you get started in your faith? Why do you go to church? What do you really believe about God?
- What are the most difficult questions you've been asked by non-believers? As a group, try to offer them answers.
- Jesus often answered a question with another question. What questions might you put to your non-believing friend?

14 'He hath a daily beauty'

- As suggested in the chapter, list your own 'hall of fame', the people who especially impressed you on your road to faith. What were the aspects of their lives that made such an impression?
- Who is your favourite biblical character, and why? If you think about it, does that person act in any way as a model or a continuing influence on you?
- Who are the special people of faith who stand out for you today? How can you support or encourage them?
- What kind of qualities would you like to develop so that God could use you to encourage the next generation?

15 'Entranced by his company'

- What do you think it was about Jesus that particularly arrested people? Try not to answer with the hindsight of faith but as if you were a contemporary encountering this Galilean preacher for the first time. Are those the same features that attract you?
- Are there aspects of Jesus' character and ministry that might have alarmed you or made you keep a distance?

- How could Jesus be both human and divine? What words, images or descriptions help you to understand this? Do you tend to start from above ('God became man') or from below ('a man totally open to God')?
- Are there parts of the Gospel accounts of Jesus at which you baulk, which you're not sure you believe? Does it help enquirers to know you have such doubts?

16 'Who speaks for the poor?'

- How do you think the contemporary Church is seen by society? For example, is it respected as a provider of social critique and care for the poor and marginalized, or as a regressive organization out of touch with the modern world and its dilemmas?
- Can you think of examples of where the Church has been in the forefront of social change in recent decades, and where it has failed to rise to particular challenges?
- What contribution to the common good and the well-being of the community does your own church make? Is such work a shared vision or the enthusiasm of a few? Does it matter?
- How can the local church, or your group, or you as an individual, engage with the global issues of our day – terrorism, climate change, migration, poverty?

17 'Let it be'

- Do you recognize either the experience of 'letting go' or of surprise in your own faith journey or that of someone you know?
- Do you sometimes 'go back to the frontier to argue with the border guards on both sides'? Have your arguments changed over the years?
- Do you tend to think of God working in our lives more from 'outside in' or from 'inside out'? Do you think of him more as 'coming towards us' or 'disclosing himself from within'?

- Identify some of the 'change of mind' or 'surprise' stories in the Bible (there are a lot more than the fishermen on the beach, Zacchaeus and Paul!). What are the unique features of each?

18 'So what?'

- Should Christians concentrate more on *clarity* or on *mystery* in speaking of God in the modern world? What are the advantages and disadvantages of both?
- If the Church were more in 'receive' mode than 'transmit', what would it hear society saying about the Church and the Christian faith today?
- 'The Word became flesh and lived among us.' If that is the 'scent' that God has laid down, how can you personally and your local church encourage people to pick up the scent of Jesus?
- 'So what' will you do as a result of all the talking in the group?

Notes

1 'Is there more to life than meets the eye?'

1 Brian Mountford, *Christian Atheist* (Winchester: O-Books, 2011), p. 3.
2 Francis Spufford, *Unapologetic* (London: Faber and Faber, 2012), p. 5.
3 Linda Woodhead, *Church Times*, 10 February 2012.
4 Source untraced.
5 Rowan Williams, *Silence and Honeycakes* (Oxford: Lion, 2003), p. 22.

2 'Is that it?'

1 Source untraced.
2 William Shakespeare, *Macbeth*, Act 5, Scene 5.
3 Tom Benyon, *Blog 2015: It's All Going South*.
4 Quoted in Benyon, *Blog 2015*, day 20.
5 Dave Tomlinson, *How To Be a Bad Christian* (London: Hodder and Stoughton, 2013), p. 193.
6 Letter to Harrison Blake, 27 March 1848.

3 'All you could desire'

1 Source untraced.
2 Quoted in Brian Mountford, *Christian Atheist* (Winchester: O-Books, 2011), p. 48.
3 Quoted by Camilla Cavendish, *Sunday Times*, 13 July 2014.
4 St Augustine, *Confessions* (various editions).
5 *The Times*, 16 May 2015.
6 C. S. Lewis, *Surprised by Joy* (London: Geoffrey Bles, 1955), p. 22
7 St Augustine, *Confessions*.

4 'Life couldn't hold any more'

1 Roger Bannister, *Twin Tracks* (London: The Robson Press, 2014), Preface.

2 Quoted in Jon Winokur, *Writers on Writing* (Philadelphia, PA: Running Press, 1986).
3 Thomas Merton, *The Seven Storey Mountain* (various editions).
4 Belden Lane, *The Solace of Fierce Landscapes* (Oxford: Oxford University Press, 1998).
5 Barbara Ehrenreich, *Living with a Wild God: A Non-believer's Search for the Truth About Everything* (London: Granta, 2015), p. 237.
6 Walt Whitman, from *Leaves of Grass* (1856).
7 Ehrenreich, *Living with a Wild God*, p. 115.
8 John V. Taylor, *A Matter of Life and Death* (London: SCM, 1986), p. 18.

5 'Earth's crammed with heaven'

1 William Blake, *The Letters* (1799).
2 G. K. Chesterton, 'Ecclesiastes', from *The White Knight and Other Poems* (London: Grant Richards, 1900).
3 William Wordsworth, 'I wandered lonely as a cloud' (various anthologies).
4 e.e. cummings, '[in Just-][in-Just]' (various anthologies).
5 A. S. Byatt, *The Biographer's Tale* (London: Chatto and Windus, 2000).
6 Gerald Manley Hopkins, 'Comments on the Spiritual Exercises of St Ignatius Loyola', *Poems* (Oxford: Oxford University Press, 1963), p. 263.
7 Alice Walker, *The Color Purple* (various editions).
8 Mother Julian of Norwich, *Revelations of Divine Love* (various editions), chapter 5.
9 Elizabeth Barrett Browning, from 'Aurora Leigh', in D. H. S. Nicholson and A. H. E. Lee (eds), *The Oxford Book of English Mystical Verse* (Oxford: Oxford University Press, 1917).
10 Jane Fonda, *Rolling Stone* magazine (June 2007).
11 Kenneth Grahame, *The Wind in the Willows* (London: Methuen, 1908).
12 Gerald Manley Hopkins, 'Pied Beauty', from *Poems* (1918).

6 'Nobody's perfect'

1 Francis Spufford, *Unapologetic* (London: Faber and Faber, 2012), p. 28.

2 Leonard Cohen, 'Anthem'.

3 Martin Luther King Jr, *A Testament of Hope* (London: HarperOne, 2003).

4 Quoted in Dallas Willard, *A Place for Truth* (Downers Grove, IL: IVP, 2010).

5 George Orwell, 'Notes on the Way', in *Time and Tide* (1940).

6 Sinead O'Connor, *Daily Telegraph*, 2 August 2014.

7 Oscar Wilde, *Lady Windermere's Fan*.

7 'Hell and high water'

1 Elie Wiesel, *Night* (London: Bantam Books, 1960), p. 62.

2 Stephen Fry, *The Meaning of Life*, RTE television, 1 February 2015.

3 Barbara Brown Taylor, *An Altar in the World* (Norwich: Canterbury Press, 2014), pp. 57, 60.

4 Etty Hillesum, *An Interrupted Life: The Diaries and Letters of Etty Hillesum 1941–1943* (London: Persephone Books, 1999), p. 355.

5 Hillesum, *An Interrupted Life*, p. 203.

6 C. S. Lewis, *The Four Loves* (London: Geoffrey Bles, 1960), p. 111.

7 Source untraced.

8 Mother Julian, *Revelations of Divine Love*, chapter 68.

8 'Don't just do something, sit there'

1 Barbara Brown Taylor, *When God is Silent* (Norwich: Canterbury Press, 2013), p. 23.

2 Source untraced.

3 Larry Culliford, *The Psychology of Spirituality* (London: Jessica Kingsley, 2011), p. 70.

4 Friedrich von Hügel, *Letters to a Niece* (Regent College, 2001), Letter 16.

5 R. S. Thomas, from *The Collected Later Poems, 1988–2000* (Newcastle upon Tyne: Bloodaxe Books, 2004). Permission to reproduce sought.

6 Elizabeth Gilbert, *Eat, Pray, Love* (London: Penguin, 2006).

9 'Tell it slant'

1 Bel Mooney, *Devout Sceptics* (London: Hodder and Stoughton, 2003), p. 7.

2 Source untraced.

3 Source untraced, quoted in Dore Ashton, *A Fable of Modern Art* (Berkeley: University of California Press, 1991), p. 93.

4 'How does art work?' *Time*, 6 July 2015, p. 67.

5 Richard Dawkins, *The God Delusion* (London: Bantam Books, 2006), p. 86.

6 *The Spectator*, 15 November 2014.

7 Jeanette Winterson, essay in Antonia Fraser (ed.), *The Pleasure of Reading* (London: Bloomsbury, 1992), p. 248.

8 Quoted in Brian Mountford, *Christian Atheist* (Winchester: O-Books, 2011), p. 36.

9 Seamus Heaney, *The Redress of Poetry* (London: Faber and Faber, 1995), p. xv.

10 Rumi, *The Essential Rumi* (San Francisco: HarperOne, 1995), p. 36.

11 Quoted in Kenneth Leech, *True Prayer* (London: Sheldon Press, 1980), p. 10.

12 Michael Mayne, *This Sunrise of Wonder* (London: HarperCollins, 1995), p. 193.

10 'Coming home'

1 Camilla Cavendish, *Sunday Times*, 13 July 2014.

2 Allison Pearson, *Daily Telegraph*, 16 February 2012.

3 Linda Woodhead, *Church Times*, July 2015.

4 Philip Larkin, *Collected Poems* (London: Faber and Faber, 2003). Reproduced with permission of Faber and Faber Ltd.

11 'Why is there something rather than nothing?'

1 Remark made on a visit to Princeton University in April 1921.

2 John Polkinghorne, *One World: The Interaction of Science and Theology* (London: SPCK, 1986), p. 80.

3 Ted Harrison, 'New Universes mean new ideas about God', *Church Times*, 24 July 2015.

4 Howard Jacobson, *The Reader*, no. 29, Spring 2008 (Liverpool University Press), p. 30.

5 Frank Dyson, 'Energy and the Universe', *Scientific American*, 225 (1971), p. 59.

6 David Bohm (1917–92), theoretical physicist.

7 Quoted in B. N. Kursunoglu and E. P. Wigner (eds), *Paul Adrien Maurice Dirac: Reminiscences about a Great Physicist* (Cambridge: Cambridge University Press, 1990), p. xv.

8 The vicar was the Revd Graham Sykes.

9 Paul Davies, from a conversation recorded in Bel Mooney, *Devout Sceptics* (London: Hodder and Stoughton, 2003), p. 57.

10 Source untraced.

11 Stephen Hawking, *A Brief History of Time* (London: Bantam Books, 1990), p. 174.

12 'Darkness at noon'

1 Rowan Williams, *Silence and Honeycakes* (Oxford: Lion, 2003), p. 10.

2 Quoted in Sheila Cassidy, *Sharing the Darkness* (London: Darton, Longman and Todd, 1992).

3 Williams, *Silence and Honeycakes*, p. 19.

13 'Hatching, matching, dispatching'

1 Caitlin Moran, *Sunday Times* magazine, 8 March 2014.

2 Albert Camus, *The Stranger*, chapter 5.

3 Source untraced.

4 Bear Grylls, *Big Issue*, 22 June 2015.

5 'On death', *Sobornost* 1.2 (1979).

14 'He hath a daily beauty'

1 William Shakespeare, *Othello*, Act 5, Scene 1.

2 *The Week*, 16 August 2014.

3 Rowan Williams, in Rowan Williams and Joan Chittister, *For All That Has Been, Thanks* (London: Canterbury Press, 2010), p. 68.

15 'Entranced by his company'

1 Susannah Butler, *Evening Standard*, 20 March, 2014.

2 John Milton, *Paradise Lost*, Book 3.

3 Malcolm Guite, *Word in the Wilderness* (Norwich: Canterbury Press, 2014), p. 8.

4 Jaroslav Pelikan, *Jesus through the Centuries* (New Haven: Yale University Press, 1985), p. 1.

5 Robert Powell, *The Sun*, January 1976.
6 C. S. Lewis, *The Lion, the Witch and the Wardrobe* (various editions).
7 David Grieve, priest-poet. Reproduced with permission.
8 Lord Hailsham, *The Door Wherein I Went* (London: Collins, 1975), pp. 54–5.

16 'Who speaks for the poor?'

1 Baroness Warsi, House of Lords debate.
2 Lord Glasman at College of Bishops meeting, Oxford 2013. An introduction to the background to his thinking can be found, via Wikipedia, from Anglia Ruskin University Symposium, November 2012.
3 George Monbiot, *The Guardian*, 17 June 2015.
4 Barry Lopez, *Arctic Dreams: Imagination and Desire in a Northern Landscape* (New York: Bantam Books, 1986), p. 250.
5 Widely quoted on the internet.
6 Barack Obama, *Dreams from My Father* (London: Canongate, 2008).
7 Charles Clarke, *The Tablet*, 28 January 2010.
8 Robert Putnam and David Campbell, *American Grace* (New York: Simon Schuster, 2010).

17 'Let it be'

1 C. S. Lewis, *Surprised by Joy* (London: Geoffrey Bles, 1955), p. 212.
2 Lewis, *Surprised by Joy*, p. 215.
3 Larry Culliford, *The Psychology of Spirituality* (London: Jessica Kingsley, 2011), p. 57.
4 See <www.scimednet.org>, <www.noetic.org>, <www.templeton.org>.
5 David Hay, *Scottish Journal of Healthcare Chaplaincy*, vol. 5, no. 1 (2002), p. 4.
6 D. H. Lawrence, from *Last Poems* (1929).

18 'So what?'

1 Rowan Williams, *Silence and Honeycakes* (Oxford: Lion, 2003).
2 Julie Burchill, *The Spectator*, 3 November 2014.
3 Howard Jacobson, University Sermon, Oxford, 13 June 2010.
4 Mike Riddell, source untraced.

5 Sarah Winman, *When God was a Rabbit* (London: Headline, 2011), p. 141.

6 Richard Rohr, *Hope against Darkness* (Cincinnati, OH: St Anthony Messenger Press, 2002).

7 Michael Rosen, *We're Going on a Bear Hunt* (London: Walker Books, 1989).

8 George Herbert, from *The Oxford Book of Christian Verse* (Oxford: The Clarendon Press, 1940).

9 Lord Hailsham, *A Sparrow's Flight* (London: Collins, 1990), p. 452.